Esprit de Corps

Esprit de Corps

A SCOTS GUARDS OFFICER
ON ACTIVE SERVICE
1943–1945

W. A. ELLIOTT

MICHAEL RUSSELL

First published in Great Britain 1996
by Michael Russell (Publishing) Ltd
Wilby Hall, Wilby, Norwich NR16 2JP

Reprinted 1996

Typeset in Sabon by The Typesetting Bureau,
Allen House, East Borough, Wimborne, Dorset
Printed and bound in Great Britain
by Biddles Ltd, Guildford and King's Lynn

Contents

	Foreword	7
1	Joining the Battalion	10
2	The Invasion	21
3	The Other Side of the Hill	41
4	Back to the Battalion	55
5	Hospital Interlude	78
6	Along the Garigliano	85
7	Back to Training	102
8	The German Frontier	108
9	Advance into Germany	121
10	The Last Battle	135
	Index	149

Foreword

Some explanation is required of how this war journal came to be kept and why it should now be published fifty years after the events it records. It was first started following a week behind the enemy lines in Italy in September 1943. It then seemed that some record of this and subsequent events might be of interest to family and friends. Such a diary, however, could not for security reasons be kept in the front line. So the events were recorded in notebooks kept with my kit behind the line, using pseudonyms for persons and military units. When my battalion temporarily returned home from Italy in April 1944 these notes were then written up into one volume with another complete volume covering the subsequent invasion of Germany. The whole was then typed up with the introduction of my impressions on first joining the battalion in North Africa. From time to time the complete journal was later lent to friends and relatives to read.

The decision to publish came about recently when a former brother officer sent me a draft of a section of his personal memoirs which he was publishing for private circulation – including his own wartime experiences in the same battalion. So I sent him my journal for information. This then led him and other retired ex-officers with whom he was in correspondence to suggest that my journal should also be published.

If I had not kept this detailed log or diary at the time I would not, after fifty years, have remembered many of the details. But with the passage of time one has perhaps become more aware of the significance of group identities and of the corresponding need to control human warfare.

This journal, however, merely records from a junior platoon officer's viewpoint how the war then appeared to him personally within an infantry battalion with which he became closely identified. It is thus a psychological as well as a military record. In particular, it records the bonds which come to be forged when one puts one's life into the hands of others and they entrust their lives to oneself. The resulting sense of identity also helps to maintain morale despite the sheer attrition of prolonged fighting in an overfought infantry battalion. This may provide some clue as to the origin of national identities which in turn were how we all came to be fighting in the first place.

For publication it has been necessary to divide the journal into separate chapters and to delete most of the dates. It was also advisable to have the text checked for inaccuracies; to insert the exact numbers of casualties as now taken from regimental records; and to ensure that the book contains nothing unnecessarily offensive to my old regiment. As so many years have now elapsed, the real names of persons and units have also been substituted, whenever possible, in lieu of the original pseudonyms.

I am greatly indebted to the following former officers of my regiment for certain corrections and suggestions: Major-General Sir John Swinton, KVCO, one-time fellow platoon officer and later commanding the Household Division; Major-General Sir Digby Raeburn, KCVO, my former company commander and later Chief of Staff Allied Forces Northern Europe; Major Alastair Ritchie; and, finally, to General Sir Michael Gow, GCB, later C-in-C BAOR and Commander NATO Northern Army Group who, above all, was responsible for arranging the publication.

The reader may be surprised to find that the journal is not particularly anti-German. Indeed one grew to respect the German Army as military opponents and they certainly treated me well enough when I was briefly their prisoner. After the war was over and I was awaiting demobilisation in Germany, I ran brigade welfare services at Lubeck in northern Germany. This involved a large German staff who proved loyal and efficient. Any previous anti-German (but not anti-Nazi) feelings therefore soon evaporated – even at a time when there was an official ban on fraternisation. In any case my job could hardly have been done except by getting on with them.

Most wartime soldiers, conscripted like myself, had never enjoyed any previous regimental identity. This was only subsequently acquired. When called up for military service half-way through the Second World War, I certainly intended to join a Scottish regiment; but I had no family connections whatsoever with the Scots Guards and only came to sign up with them by chance as a friend happened to be doing so.

The publication of this journal has thus been undertaken not only as a military record but also because it happens to provide a contemporary case history of how human identities (with their consequent loyalties) can be created and retained. As such it may even provide some lessons for the control of human warfare and the furtherance of international peacekeeping.

Joining the Battalion

I arrived as a new boy on 12 August 1943 to find most of the 2nd Battalion Scots Guards out on manoeuvres. The sweltering sun beat down upon their almost vacant encampment, one of many that lined the hill ground above Tripoli where citrus plantations, maintained by constant irrigation, petered out amid the surrounding desert. All living growth was parched brown except beside the water channels. Whirling sprays were watering the grapefruit trees as my newly allocated orderly found a dry one to which he tethered my tent ropes despite the frenzied objections of the Arab farmer. 'Never mind the wogs, sir,' he advised me as he spread out my kit and went off to find another old soldier, the Quartermaster-Sergeant, who presided over the dark interior of the nearby store tent.

When I had settled my things I went over to join them. It was scorching hot outside. Within the tent a group of the Quartermaster-Sergeant's cronies were concealed, swapping stories of the past desert campaign. During most of it my orderly had been looking after some dug-away officer on the Cairo staff; but he nevertheless managed to keep his end up with the other old campaigners as if he had been in all the Battalion's battles from the early days at Mersa Matruh. They were a choice bunch of rogues, now safely ensconced in Company Headquarters and stores. Their main preoccupation on campaign, judging from their conversation, appeared to have been the acquisition of loot. I could not get them to talk much about the actual fighting (of which at one time they had done their share) but with glittering eyes they told me of 'the bags of loot' they had been able to gather following the Battalion's last attack at Hammamet with the final German surrender at Cape Bon. This was when von Arnim capitulated with the remnants of the German Afrika Korps, thereby ending three years' fighting in North Africa. From all accounts the Battalion had then been able to acquire a considerable haul of German Luger pistols which had been promptly turned into dollars with the newly arrived American Forces.

My orderly asked the Quartermaster-Sergeant whether he still had a spare revolver for his 'officer bloke', but his entire selection had already been converted into American dollars. I did not really mind however, as I was already a practised shot with my own Webley pistol – which, I was assured, was less likely to jam than a German automatic. I had used it to pot petrol tins all the way along the North African coast.

The fresh breezes of evening carried the sound of the pipes playing my new battalion back to camp. I stood by the side of the track and watched them marching in by platoons and companies; suntanned and fit, they looked among the toughest troops I had ever seen. Then I went into the officers' mess tent of a company to which I was temporarily attached as supernumerary pending a vacant platoon of my own. I felt supernumerary in every sense of the word and quite out of place among this foreign body of men who, conditioned by the desert fighting, had acquired not only a range of idiosyncrasies but a different sense of values.

The company officers came into the tent one by one for a drink after dismissing their platoons for the night. Nobody appeared to have warned anybody else of my temporary attachment; but the company commander was affable enough and offered me a whisky before donning an immaculate gabardine service dress, made in Cairo, and disappearing down to Tripoli for dinner with some other officers in Brigade Headquarters. The remainder of us settled down for the evening. The conversation revolved round, rather than included me, for my attempted contribution about new weapons and battle drills was obviously regarded as taking the war too seriously. There was talk of the recent Battle of Hammamet and how some of the Battalion's anti-tank gunners had got at the enemy's supply of *vino* – with dire results; how the Battalion had afterwards guarded a prison camp at Sousse containing many of their old desert opponents – the German 90th Light Division; and of the party they had one night there in the German officers' mess with an officer called Rudi who sang 'Lilli Marlene' and other German songs. Also how during the previous campaign one of our men, nicknamed 'Parachute Pete', had succeeded while on patrol in capturing a flag of the same 90th Light. The Germans in turn had one night managed to infiltrate the neighbouring officers' latrines.

In retrospect it all sounded very sporting but I felt out of my depth, being unaccustomed to view the national enemy as just an opposing team of old soldiers. Still fairly fresh from a Britain where we regarded each bomb dropped as an outrage and the Nazi aggressors as the slayers of innocent women and children, I still retained my civilian belief that we were engaged in a life and death struggle for democracy and the freedom of the world. Yet here I found this struggle treated more as an incident in regimental history against a reasonably sporting opponent.

And so, day by day, this jocular but professional attitude to fighting (for they thought little of the war in general) had to be accepted as one sat in the officers' mess tent in the evenings, while the desert night came down and the sudden cooling of the sands sent the breezes rushing out to sea. While the lamp swayed crazily from the tent-pole and the canvas sides reverberated with careless laughter, the talk of these fighting men had little to do with war aims or what we were supposed to be fighting for. Nor did it seem to pay particular respect to our 'glorious dead'. These were referred to in 8th Army parlance as having been 'brewed up'. 'Brewing up' was originally the term applied to the British Tommy's universal habit in the desert of making tea at every halt over a tin filled with an ignited mixture of sand and petrol. Then when a tank was set on fire by the enemy this also became referred to as 'a brew up'. Now the expression was applied nonchalantly to the deaths of one's best friends – 'Poor old John got himself brewed up, sticking his head out of an O.P. at Enfidaville.'

The *esprit de corps* of the old desert 8th Army in which they served – given a new impetus under the victorious generalship of 'Monty' (Field-Marshal Montgomery) – was intense. With the exception of the 'Forgotten' 14th Army in Burma, these 'Desert Rats' were perhaps the only British Army formation to acquire a strong identity of their own – for a soldier's loyalty does not usually extend beyond his division. But in its isolated situation, fighting with its back to the wall with no other Allied troops at first involved, the 8th Army had obviously grown very conscious of itself as a *corps d'elite*. So much so that all outsiders, even British soldiers like myself posted recently from home, were regarded as strangers. We were referred to in derogatory terms as 'Inglese' – the Egyptian word for English. In the 8th Army an officer dressed for war in true cavalier fashion with silk neckscarf, suede desert boots, yellow or pink shirt from Mahommed's in Cairo and all his webbing equipment blancoed white; none of this camouflage nonsense! To the keen Britain-based soldier the uniform (if such it could be called) of these 'sandmen' appeared foppish and unmilitary. Perhaps some of them did need to shake the sand out of their desert boots and recognise that there were other virtues than to have been at Medenine. Nevertheless they had also come to disregard some of the duller and more tiresome military conventions that serve no real purpose and tend to stifle initiative and adventure.

These veterans of 201 Guards Brigade were certainly 'characters'. It was apparent from now talking to them that they had gained a healthy respect for their military opponents, the German Afrika Korps, and its commander General Rommel. Perhaps it was only natural under the peculiar conditions of desert fighting, with soldiers confronting each other in the absence of civilian fanaticism, that they should come to have some regard for the other side and to respect the unwritten military code of what was and what was not 'good form' in the practice of warfare. With the exception of the Italians (or so it was said) both sides appeared to have fought 'correctly'. Perhaps it paid them to do so and to realise that, unlike their respective civilian populations, they were all in the Desert War together. As reported in the press, this feeling was carried to high levels. After his capture at Sidi Rezegh, General von Ravenstein was hospitably received by General Auchinleck. The former wrote a letter of congratulations to his adversary, Major-General Campbell, who had just been awarded the VC: 'The German comrades congratulate you with warm heart on your award.' After Alamein, General Montgomery even invited the captured General von Thoma to breakfast, thereby invoking an outcry in the British press. The chivalry of General Rommel was a byword on both sides of the firing line.

One of the old guardsmen who had just accompanied me on convoy along the North African coast told me how Rommel had visited the hospital in which he lay wounded and which had been temporarily overrun. The German general asked after his health as if he had been one of his own privates.

All this chivalry and sportsmanship – more like international competitive sports – was of course quite alien to the feelings of national antagonism among the civilian populations back home, infuriated by bombing casualties and the distant slaughter of their sons.

The real enemy of these 8th Army veterans seemed to have been the hard campaigning conditions; and their main endeavour the struggle to maintain the name and fighting efficiency of the Battalion and the Regiment despite the constant drain of casualties. There were only some hundred guardsmen now left of the original battalion of 800 that on the outbreak of war in 1939 had been stationed in Cairo. They had to wait until 1941 for the first shots to be fired – against the Italians. Since then the fighting had been deadly and continuous. I had just motored from Cairo along the North African coast with a group of reinforcements through the Battalion's old battlefields – and seen their graveyards. At Sollum we had seen the 1,000-foot escarpment in front of the Italian fort which they had scaled by night and had then burst in on a vastly superior force in a bayonet charge that earned them the nickname over the Italian radio of 'the butchers of Sollum'. Their other main battles had been at Sidi Rezegh, El Agheila and Rigel Ridge, where part of the Battalion (armed with puny 2-pounder anti-tank guns) were overrun.

Their greatest feat of arms, however, had been recently in March 1943 at Medenine when Rommel launched his armoured counterattack on the 8th Army's Mareth Line. The whole weight of the German attack had descended on 201 Guards Brigade, armed now with 6-pounder (instead of 2-pounder) anti-tank guns backed by field artillery. When the Germans later withdrew they left fifty-three tanks knocked out, fifteen on the Battalion's own front, destroyed by the Battalion's anti-tank guns. Some of the latter had been secured on the backs of 3-ton lorries firing over open sights as the tanks topped the ridge in front.

Such then was the fighting background and reputation of this overfought battalion I had come to join. It was also the background of the 2nd Battalion Coldstream Guards in 201 Guards Brigade who had shared the same experiences the whole way through. The 6th Battalion Grenadier Guards had only recently joined in Syria. There nevertheless appeared to be a whole brigade as well as a separate battalion *esprit de corps*. It was doubtless such feelings that made these veterans disdainful of outsiders like myself until we had been adopted within their close fraternity. Like all newcomers to the Battalion, I resented their attitude and at first found much to disapprove of. In particular I felt worried by their seeming lack of keenness to continue fighting. Indeed I was aghast at the apparently low morale of some of the older soldiers which I had been misled to believe was impossible in the Brigade of Guards. In the company to which I had just been posted I even found two veteran sergeants and some guardsmen under arrest for near-mutiny. They had all been abroad since 1939 and had now seized some Battalion trucks and driven off along the coast on a holiday spree when they heard they were not after all to be allowed home at the conclusion of the North African campaign. The general feeling was that the Battalion should be repatriated for a well-earned rest and someone else be made to do their share of fighting.

I suppose there is a limit to the amount a man can stand of being under fire, wounded, patched up and then returned to the battlefront, and still retain his keenness. The Battalion, like the now battle-weary 7th Armoured and Highland Divisions, were no longer so keen as they once were. But this did not lessen their sense of distinction or their determination to prevent outsiders taking their unit's name in vain.

There had been rumours, when I first set out in military convoy from Cairo to join this battalion, that they were about to be sent home, along with some other old desert units. So strong were these rumours that some dug-aways, like my orderly and the ex-wounded who could have decently prolonged their convalescence, had even come speeding back on the frank admission that it was only to avoid getting left behind when the Battalion left for home. To my personal relief now came the bombshell news that, despite its long spell of active service, the Battalion and the Brigade were not going home after all. As seasoned infantry they were required to support a new 'Second Front' on the European continent which, despite the recent ending of the North African and Sicilian campaigns, was required immediately to relieve the heavy German pressure on the Russians. Our brigade was therefore now to join the 56th (London) Division as part of 10 Corps to form a new American 5th Army under an American general, Mark Clark. Our senior officers refused at first to substitute for their old Desert Rat sign the Black Cat of the 56th (London) Divison. One transport driver who did so was stopped by the Commanding Officer and asked whether he would like a bowl of milk! The American divisions were all brand new and the two British infantry divisions had but lately been blooded in Tunisia.

The British Corps Commander, in a pep talk to our brigade of-ficers, said he had applied for, and been allocated, our brigade of seasoned infantry which he expected to be in the forefront of the initial assault. The compliment, if intended as such, fell on deaf ears so far as the older soldiers were concerned. When I had to convey the news of the pending assault landing to those men who had just ac-companied me from Cairo in the expectation of going home, they were visibly shaken. One sergeant said, 'It's all right for you, sir, you're just out from home. I was as keen as you when I first went in with the boys at Sollum and a finer battalion you never saw. That's when I caught my first packet. Then I was with Major Macrae, the finest officer and gentleman I ever knew. He was killed at El Taqa when I caught it again – in the leg this time. I got my last wound at Mareth. The older boys like me, sir, can't go on. It's someone else's turn.'

This then was the general atmosphere I encountered, although understandable in view of the Battalion's long fighting record. But, like other keen young officers recently joined, I found it somewhat depressing. Not yet feeling I belonged, I could not as yet share their feelings.

After a few days with the Battalion, however, it became apparent that they were settling down to the prospect of fresh action and steeling themselves to the likelihood of more heavy casualties. *Esprit de corps* demanded that the name of *the* Battalion and *the* Regiment be maintained in the face not only of the enemy but also of rival regiments. That could only be if they accepted the situation and settled down to reorganisation and training. The stronger discipline too, now reimposed by officers and NCOs, also helped in the preparation and training when, if full scope had been allowed to individual feelings, the Battalion spirit might have disintegrated. The older men, already trained in the Regular Army, were also extremely smart when they wanted to be. So, despite the undercurrent of battle-weariness, we made a fine sight marching through Tripoli with our pressed khaki drill shorts, our anklets, belts and rifle slings all blancoed white, our brasses gleaming and the Battalion pipe band playing bravely at our head. It gave me, at any rate, my first feelings of really belonging.

Back in my company officers' mess the pending invasion was now being referred to, in public school fashion, with some jocularity. It was known as 'the bloodbath' and anyone who had been fortunate enough to escape so far would have 'had it' in a few weeks' time. There were two brothers nicknamed 'the Bull' and 'the Dog' who bet each other that they would be 'brewed up' first. There was much laughter too at the prospects of a certain supernumerary officer whose job it apparently was to go in with the commandos and reconnoitre our positions. He was certain to get 'brewed up'!

My presence in 'G' Company was only temporary, for two days

after my arrival I was posted permanently to Right Flank Company, so-called because in days of yore they always held the right of the line. They regarded themselves as the crack company of the Battalion and tried to maintain their position to the prejudice of others – but it was some weeks before I could become conscious of them being 'my' company.

A week after my arrival, one of Right Flank's officers went down with the prevalent malaria and a platoon was thereby freed for my command. The lives of thirty individuals thus became my own responsibility; and they started to become – in the deepest possessive sense – my platoon. But I felt my way to start with, for they were a mixed bunch of old soldiers as well as new reinforcements and I did not wish to offend the former with any new ideas on battle tactics deriving from the battle school at Barnard Castle. After a few days' training, however, I found they did not respond unkindly to these 'battle drills' designed for close-country fighting. The open desert manoeuvres to which they were more accustomed had been very different and hardly involved separate platoon tactics – except on night patrol. In the desert, moreover, the 2nd Battalion Scots Guards (referred to in orders as 2SG) had been motorised infantry conveyed in trucks and with an unusual armament of anti-tank guns and heavy machine-guns. Now, apart from the 6-pounder anti-tank guns, these heavy weapons and motor transport were removed and everyone had to get used to being foot-slogging infantry again. Some regarded the removal of most of our vehicles as involving loss of status and everyone, from the Commanding Officer downwards refused to part with their motor battalion black berets worn with the regimental cap star in the middle.

Our training as foot-slogging infantry now became increasingly vigorous as there was only a week or two left before 'the bloodbath'. The first part of this had been mainly physical, to get the men as hard as nails. It consisted of PT, route marches carrying all equipment and bathing afterwards in the Mediterranean. How we loathed those route marches! But bronzed by the sun the physique of the men looked magnificent. Then followed section training conducted by platoon officers like myself with three infantry sections to each platoon of about thirty men each. Next came weapon training with all three platoons learning to use their Bren light machine-guns and 2-inch mortars as covering fire while the rest of the riflemen advanced to attack imaginary German positions. Then ensued exercises at company level involving all three platoons, comprising about 100 men in all. Each company was commanded by a major, with a captain as second-in-command.

It soon became apparent that the veterans were correct to be critical of some aspects of the new British battle school tactics then in vogue which treated close-country fighting as if on a drill parade. I realised even then that I had much to learn from the older NCOs about the practical side of war.

After this company training was over there followed battalion manoeuvres involving all four rifle companies, namely Right Flank, 'F', 'G' and Left Flank; also Headquarter Company containing the battalion signals and transport vehicles and Support Company with the 3-inch mortars, 6-pounder anti-tank guns and carrier platoons. The whole battalion on manoeuvres involved about 800 men in all. On the final day of our preliminary training in the Tripolitanian desert, with the temperature over 100 degrees in the shade and each man carrying a 60 lb load, we had a fifteen-mile march ending with a mock assault on a hilltop Arab village. Many of the men were by then prostrated with exhaustion; but we had been warned to be prepared on landing to carry all our kit for forty-eight hours without motor transport.

The final stage of our training was a practice landing from assault craft further down the coast, involving not only 201 Guards Brigade but also the other two brigades of the 56th (London) Division to which we were now attached. This, however, resulted in a mix up and some troops were even off-loaded on a sand bar out at sea.

Shortly thereafter all our heavy kit and battalion transport were loaded onto landing ships (LSTs) in Tripoli harbour and it became apparent that our days in North Africa were now numbered. The enemy must also have realised this for there were some lively bombing raids over Tripoli harbour, in one of which the popular Corps Commander, General Horrocks, was badly wounded and was replaced by General McCreery. Otherwise there was no hitch in the last-minute preparations for the invasion.

Our Commanding Officer, Colonel Guy Taylor (it was regimental custom to refer to senior officers only by their Christian name), gave a pep talk to the assembled Battalion just before we embarked. This was very much as if we were a football team facing the big match. Colonel Guy said just the right things about the spirit of the Battalion and our ability to beat the enemy. Indeed, with all the officers sitting in a row out in front, the scene reminded one painfully of one's schooldays. I even found myself eyeing with jealousy the small purple and white (MC) ribbons above the shirt pockets of some of the older officers and hoping that I too might be able to earn this adult military version of one's school colours

Colonel Guy had commanded Support Company at the recent Battle of Medenine and had been decorated for bravery for towing one of his guns out in front of our lines to knock out two of the many German tanks then attacking the Battalion. He had all the advantages and drawbacks of intense personal charm and, in his attitude to his brother officers, seemed more of an overgrown company commander than a commanding officer. The older soldiers, however, all regarded him as their hero. Now, standing before us for his pep talk, dressed in immaculately pressed khaki drill trousers, silk neckscarf and black beret, he seemed to typify that easy assumption of superiority, that dandyism, individuality and disregard for the duller military conventions that typifed the old 8th Army and 201 Guards Brigade in particular.

The new Brigadier, on the other hand, was a more conventional soldier and guardsman and very different to Colonel Guy. The two of them, in consequence, did not see eye to eye.

I spent the last few days before embarkation getting to know my new platoon individually. They were mainly Scottish, with a number from London and Liverpool where the Regiment also had recruiting offices. I found it easiest to get to know them through their leavening of keen young soldiers just arrived from home as reinforcements from the recently disbanded 4th Battalion of the Regiment which had already been trained in close-country fighting. Tired of the interminable exercises of Home Command, they were now as eager as myself to put all their past training into practice on live targets capable of shooting back. Like me they welcomed, if apprehensively, the impending test of battle. I found one youth concealing a malarial fever in the hopes that he would not miss going into action with his old mates from the disbanded 4th Battalion. I nevertheless had to force him protesting off to hospital.

Waiting day by day like this, knowing that any morning we might suddenly be ordered aboard, became trying on the nerves. All the flies, too, of North Africa seemed to be attracted to Tripoli by the vast concentration of troops. The latrines swarmed with them, spreading dysentery; the food on our tables had to be covered with inverted soup plates or it became inedible in the space of a minute as the myriads of flies descended from the tent roof. In the morning one had to shave under a mosquito net if the sun was up. But it was pleasant enough after sundown writing by the light of an oil lamp or watching the pyrotechnical display over Tripoli harbour as the Germans tried to bomb our assembled assault craft. When the scarlet tracers of the anti-aircraft guns had died away there would be silence again but for the grating of the crickets in the oleander trees and someone playing an accordion in the company lines. On the table in my tent I always had a vase of those most beautiful of African lilies, the pearl white amaryllis, which grew wild nearby. Their perfume hung sweet and heavy on the desert night. Below our encampment the ground sloped gradually away to a Mediterranean lit fitfully by the moon – and the occasional flashes of anti-aircraft guns.

2

The Invasion

About a week after our practice 'invasion' along the coast and three weeks after I first joined the Battalion we received, all of a sudden, orders to embark. Some thought this was yet another practice landing, but most of us realised this to be the real thing at last. However, as no orders had been given and no one knew exactly where we were bound for, conjecture was rife. Some thought Greece, some Crete, some Italy and some even the south of France. I thought the latter as Churchill had recently been talking about invading the 'soft underbelly of the Axis' – whereas Italy would present an extremely horny backside. As it turned out, Churchill had either not been speaking geographically or did not know his geography. Our landing was to be exactly where my guardsman orderly had told me it would – having gleaned this information from a military policeman! But on embarkation we were not yet supposed to know where we were going and, for security reasons, our sealed orders were only to be broken open at sea.

Embarkation was effected under cover of darkness. All night long thousands of troops from the two assault divisions were marching down the roads from their respective encampments and converging on Tripoli harbour. There we mounted the gangways into landing craft by the subdued light of flares. It was otherwise a pitch dark night but the artificial lights illuminated an Italian statue of Romulus and Remus mounted on a towering plinth beside the quay. It seemed to preside like some Roman emblem over our preparations. The night was loud with the shouts of officers and sergeants, the sound of cranes and winches; while, incongruously, from the bridge of a nearby ship came the sound of Humphrey Lyttelton (then a Grenadier) with his jazz trumpet playing the 'St Louis Blues'.

A day later, 5 September 1943, the vast convoy sailed out into the Mediterranean and we learnt that the 8th Army from Sicily had already crossed the Straits of Messina and landed in the south of Italy. Right Flank and Left Flank Companies were in one LSI (landing ship infantry) and 'F' and 'G', with battalion headquarters, in another. That meant about 250 men to each landing craft. Support and Head-quarter Companies, with all the heavy weapons and transport which had been loaded on to an LSI beforehand, were to follow in a later convoy and would not take part in the initial landings.

These landing craft were hardly designed for comfort or for long voyages. We were packed into stifling holds without bunks to sleep on – only wooden seats like French third-class railway carriages. After two full days at sea we ran into a heavy gale which turned the holds into chaos while men retched and were sick in all directions. We shipped so much water over the bows that our bread and cigarette rations stored there were saturated. It was also my twenty-first birthday. I managed to stave off sea-sickness all day by standing on deck watching the other assault craft in the convoy labouring through the heavy seas, now and again completely disappearing in clouds of spray. During my night watch on the ship's bridge the effect in complete darkness of soaring right up into the air, then sinking down again to hit the troughs of the waves with a terrific crash, was too much for my digestion.

Next morning, however, the sun shone on a calm and glistening sea. The whole convoy of ships, conveying our corps, could be seen stretching right to the horizon. We now knew that tomorrow was to be 'D-day' and that we were to land in the Gulf of Salerno just south of Naples. In the afternoon our fleet anchored off the Sicilian shore near Palermo, and waited there until another huge convoy appeared over the horizon conveying the American Assault Corps from Bizerta.

The still autumn afternoon lazed on while our convoy remained at anchor, soon to be joined by the American convoy. Waiting like this was a bit nerve-racking. For a diversion, some of us, including Colonel Guy, swam ashore and talked to some American soldiers there on the beaches. On returning aboard Colonel Guy encouraged all the men to swim around the ship to recover their fitness and the crew suspended rope ladders over the side for the purpose.

About 6 p.m. it began to get cold and we clothed ourselves. The men mostly retired to the holds which had now been swabbed clean of sea-sickness but were still malodorous. A blood red sun sank into the western sea and the enveloping twilight hid first the ships of the American corps, then the neighbouring British ships, and finally left us alone in our own LSI with only the sound of the waves lapping gently against its sides. I was feeling rather frightened now, and could not think why I had originally been so keen for such a perilous situation. Partly, I suppose, my fear was at appearing afraid tomorrow in front of my men and I had simply no idea how I would react to the supreme test of nerves – one's first battle. I wondered how I should behave if I found myself being shot at or having deliberately to aim at and shoot a fellow human being. For an assault landing like this would almost certainly involve close-combat fighting.

But whatever one's secret fears, the general atmosphere was still one of intense excitement that completely robbed one of all appetite for the last evening meal aboard. Everyone seemed stimulated and, outwardly at least, tried to keep up the pretence that they welcomed tomorrow's invasion. If some wished that the whole venture might, at the last moment, be cancelled, they did not show it.

There was nothing left to do now but rehearse again the final details of tomorrow's attack with the aid of maps and low-level aerial photographs. The general plan was for the American 5th Army (of which we formed part) to land in the Bay of Salerno at first light with an initial assault force of two British divisions to the north and one American division to the south. One other British and another American division were to follow up later. Our battle orders looked fine on paper as they only reckoned for the actual enemy then occupying the coastal area, namely Crown Prince Umberto's Italian division and a German Panzer division. The five other German divisions south of Naples, so we were told, were already concentrated opposite the British 8th Army at the toe of Italy. But there were known to be other German divisions in Northern Italy and the Italians, at least on paper, had other divisions of their own which they could put into the field.

The detailed plans for 201 Guards Brigade appeared somewhat nebulous. Out at sea, we had first been told that the Brigade was to be a floating reserve to be used where needed but with the probable role of sailing into Naples harbour to support the 82nd American Airborne Division which was to be landed by air on Naples aerodrome. This over-optimistic plan was now abandoned and we were allocated a place of landing at the mouth of the Tusciano river, right in the centre of the Bay of Salerno.

It was pitch dark when the ship's engines started up and the whole convoy began to move forward. Soon afterwards my company assembled on deck for a final briefing by our company commander. All

[23]

prepared to listen intently. Suddenly the ship's loud-hailer blared into life and announced in deep gruff tones to an astounded audience that, on the command of Field-Marshal Badoglio, the Italian Army had surrendered. This Italian Army of 35 divisions was now to spring to the aid of the victors. It looked like a last-minute walkover and shouts of 'The war's over! The war's over!' could be heard on every side. Men stumbled down the gangways to tell their sleeping mates the dramatic news. Those who had been secretly hoping for a cancellation of tomorrow's attack suddenly felt very brave again and cheated of worthy opposition. It certainly looked as if Prince Umberto's coastal units would be involved in the general Italian surrender and that the German divisions in the south could only motor north out of the trap set by the Allies timed to coincide with this Italian defection, to cause them most embarrassment.

We all congregated on deck in high spirits despite one sceptical veteran sergeant beside me who announced, 'Jerry won't let us get away with this, sir!' The sensational turn of events clearly called for celebration; moreover my twenty-first birthday had just passed unnoticed. The ship's Captain ordered 'Splice the mainbrace.' Paddy was running round saying he would capture a Fiat car on the morrow and fill it brimful of looted *vino* for the company. Then an impromptu singsong started as the rum ration went round. All the old Right Flank characters performed and the singing of their familiar and mainly scurrilous songs continued until the sudden firing of ack-ack guns out in front reminded us that there was still a war on and that it might not be such a walkover after all. It appeared that German aircraft had now located the front of our convoy as it neared the coast. The glum sergeant said, 'I told you Jerry wouldn't let us get away with it', and stumped off below deck. Others followed him and some younger men now looked apprehensive.

It was close on midnight and the fleet still steamed, more slowly now, towards the Salerno beaches. I could not sleep for excitement and was grateful when the time came for my watch on deck. There I could breathe the cool night air and see the dim shape of other ships around me lit by occasional flashes of gunfire. Sometimes the sea ahead glowed like a crimson lotus flower in the light of an enemy flare; slowly the red bloom withered and died – and all was darkness again. I did not feel so afraid now and hugged that original feeling of expectancy which men presumably feel before their first battle. Here was our war galley with myself on the bridge, heading for the Roman shore; and below deck my platoon of warriors dreamed their ancient dreams. The chill of approaching dawn was in the air when I went down to join them.

I must have been fast asleep below deck when the first assault troops landed. Apparently they did not encounter much opposition at first as some of the Italian coastal troops on the beaches had abandoned their positions. It was rumoured, however, that inland the Germans were well prepared and that they had already sent tank units forward to create a serious situation to our north.

Up on deck, it was now a glorious morning and the sun illuminated the whole magnificent panorama. An armada of ships stretched behind us to the horizon. In front the Salerno beaches still lay shrouded in mist or smoke. Our ship was still some six miles offshore and stationary. There was not a sound of battle near at hand and only occasional muffled explosions from the mainland. To our north and only a mile distant rose the steep mountains of the Sorrento peninsula with pretty fishing villages nestling at their foot. It had become quite hot and some sea birds settled on the rigging. Then the blue sky suddenly sprouted puffs of black smoke as our anti-aircraft guns opened up on high-flying German aircraft. Our men manning the Oerlikon guns (we had a brigade team) craned their necks to get a shot, but the Germans were too high and flew off unloading their bombs harmlessly in the sea.

Still no reliable news. We did learn, however, that as reserve group the Brigade was to be committed immediately in support of one of the British divisions which had been held up; but nothing more definite. We hung around in groups looking towards the shore and beginning to grow fretful.

Suddenly the booming megaphone from a control ship ordered us to beach immediately. Our landing-craft roared into life, charged in the direction of the beaches, rammed another transport, ripped off its port-side landing plank and then was ordered to stop again. We were under shellfire now - one shell hit the next-door ship - but our men settled down to sleep, weary after their long uncomfortable voyage.

Our LSI eventually beached quite peacefully at 3.30 p.m. As we made our final run in and grounded gently on the sandy foreshore it was like coming back to well-known haunts. There was the familiar mouth of the Tusciano river, the water tower and the two villas beside a wood – all familiar from our low-level air photographs. Only two ships appeared to be knocked out on 'Roger' beach but one of them, still on fire, we were later to learn, contained twelve tanks of our supporting squadron of the Scots Greys. The enemy shelling was still spasmodic – although it was to increase in intensity. My first impression was that this invasion differed little from previous manoeuvres except for the absence of staff officers acting as umpires. There also seemed to be less noise and shouting.

My company climbed up the beach and threaded its way into an area of green fields beyond. After the monochrome of the African desert the hinterland was green and beautiful and the fields glistened with crimson tomatoes and the lush leaves of tobacco plants. The peasants must have been harvesting when our attack started as piles of half-filled tomato boxes lined the roads. About twelve miles to the east great purple mountains encircled the plain, while north and south they reached within a mile of the beaches and provided the German artillery with perfect observation posts.

Right Flank marched with the rest of the Battalion to an assembly area half a mile from the beaches. Here we halted along a ditch and started to 'brew up' in 8th Army fashion. It was wonderful to be able to stretch one's legs again after being cooped up so long at sea. A gun banged away vaguely to our left. Some old soldier suggested it sounded like a German tank which only raised roars of laughter and accusations that he was 'windy'. We were still in reserve, and the invasion did not look like being a very serious affair after all: perhaps just some light opposition from units that did not yet know that Italy had surrendered. The two other battalions of our brigade which had landed earlier in the afternoon were rumoured to have been already mopping up stray Italian coastal positions.

We stopped along a hedge and whiled away the time eating apples. The evening sun was beginning to sink behind us when it became apparent from a general stirring that there was a move on. Orders were shouted. My company commander, who had been at a senior officers' conference, came back looking worried and asked us what the hell we were doing not taking up proper battle positions. We looked sheepish when informed that far from being in reserve we were in fact part of the front line, as both British divisions had been halted in their advance and forced to dig in around a narrow perimeter. 201 Guards Brigade had apparently been landed to plug a gap in the middle. But from where we were it was difficult to see what could be holding everyone up. There was not a sign of any Germans or Italians. Admittedly when one listened intently one could just hear the distant pop-popping of rifle fire or the occasional hammering of light machine-guns. But there was hardly any artillery fire nor had any of our own field guns yet been landed. I had imagined a battle to be a much more noisy affair.

The Brigadier now came past my platoon accompanied by Colonel Guy. He looked rather fierce with his red tabs and the flywhisk he always carried. I heard him saying something about 'getting a bloody move on' to Colonel Guy. Everyone's tempers seemed on edge like the Brigadier's. Hastily concocted orders were passed down the chain of command and eventually reached my company: we were to advance and get astride the Montecorvino–Battipaglia road three miles in front. The project looked feasible enough under cover of night but, as things turned out, it took an entire army corps a week to achieve.

We marched off immediately into the gathering darkness and towards our start line. I watched our company runner pushing his pedal cycle through a stream we had to cross and solemnly lugging it over hedges and ditches until he reached a stretch of pathway for a few yards' ride. He was the butt of the old 8th Army men and, in face of their laughter, seemed inclined to jettison his useless contraption. But it was part of the official complement of infantry companies, according to British home standards.

We caught up with the Brigade Commander and Colonel Guy in a farmyard just behind the forward positions. In the dim light the Brigadier still looked formidable – the embodiment of all fiery senior commanders – and I felt rather nervous being under his command, more particularly as he was nicknamed 'the Butcher' and looked as if he would willingly have us all slaughtered. Colonel Guy, in contrast, stood next to him, clothed in his usual desert boots, soft yellow shirt and black beret, with a guardsman's rifle slung over one shoulder. By his side also stood 'Blondie' Watson, MM, his orderly, and an old battalion character. They epitomised all that was best of the desert tradition. Colonel Guy's attitude was also reassuring to young officers like myself, for he was clearly 'one of us' and obviously concerned to see that we took our objectives with as few casualties as possible.

Nothing much happened as we rested in a farmyard. Suddenly a curious firework sailed screeching overhead, making everyone duck, and then landed with a bang in the hedgerow behind. This was the first enemy shell and we had clearly been observed by them. Our plan of attack was now altered. It appeared that another battalion of our brigade had run into enemy opposition just in front. We were to take over their positions at dawn when they were to attack and dislodge the enemy in front. Thereafter my battalion was to follow through and take the next objective, which was the crossroads beside a tobacco factory on the main Montecorvino to Battipaglia road. This was regarded as a key point for the control of the Salerno Plain.

There was no sleep that night as we groped our way in the dark along farm tracks to take over the Grenadiers' positions. At dawn Right Flank were stopped by one of their officers and were told to go no further as there were some hostile Italian positions just in front. We felt inclined to question this - which hardly complied with our briefing - when the sudden crack of bullets sounded close over our heads. The Grenadiers formed up for the attack along a ditch behind a tall tobacco plantation. Robert, their platoon officer, turned out to be someone I knew well from schooldays together and we had a short chat about old times. Dawn was now rising over the mountains to reveal the tired and pallid faces of our men who had not slept the night before.

It was almost broad daylight when the Grenadiers' 3-inch mortar barrage opened up on the Italian positions. Their bombs screeched over our heads and landed in flights beyond the tobacco plantation just ahead. I peered over the top of our ditch waiting for the next stage of the drama to unfold. Then the explosive shells changed to smoke as Robert's and the other two platoons of his company advanced through us to shouts of 'Good luck, lads!' from our men and 'OK, Jock, your turn next' in reply. Then the Grenadiers clambered over our ditch into the no man's land in front. I noticed one of them stoop down and pick a tomato to eat as he went. I felt deliciously safe watching them from my ditch. Soon they disappeared amidst the smoke and I could see nothing more. Then the mortar bombs stopped exploding and I heard the hammering of machine-guns and the popping of rifle fire. I could even hear an officer or sergeant shouting, 'Come on the Bill Browns!' as one might encourage a football side. Then a cheer went up as of men charging in with the bayonet. After that, a complete and ominous silence.

One man came tottering back down the road towards us, smiling in ghastly fashion with his face, neck and arms streaming vermilion blood. Out in front another man was crying, 'Help! Help!' in half-conscious anguish. The shouts came from a tobacco field and we sent our stretcher-bearers to bring him in. Apparently the attack had succeeded with few casualties, but there was nothing that could be done for poor Robert. I spoke to his sergeant who told me his officer had got a bullet through the head from the first Italian machine-gun position. I did not wish to see his body and was relieved when ordered to get ready to move immediately for it was to be our turn next; I felt rather sick.

On walking round to one of my sections largely composed of old 8th Army veterans, I found them unconcernedly brewing up and even frying bacon and eggs. I told them to pack up at once, ready to move on, but was treated to comments of 'Roll on, Joe Stalin' etc. from the disgruntled breakfasters, who still had time to consume the contents of their mess tins before cleaning and packing them away in their haversacks.

Some prisoners now appeared down the road from the newly captured Italian positions. Their appearance was incongruous and they looked more like commercial travellers, smiling and anxious to please. They also wore a curious hotchpotch of clothing and carried suitcases of belongings. An old bull-necked British sergeant started seizing the latter and shouting, 'Don't take any bloody Eyeties prisoner!' He seemed quite apopleptic and I wondered if he really meant it. However, they were escorted to the rear – minus all their belongings.

This was the only Italian opposition we were to encounter, for most Italians now appeared to have left the defence of Italy to the Germans.

The Battalion now moved on towards its appointed objectives, not yet knowing them to be a main part of the German defence line. For supporting fire we had a squadron of tanks of the Scots Greys (so called from the grey horses on which the regiment were mounted for the Battle of Waterloo). Their landing craft had not been sunk like the other one. Their tanks were American-built Shermans which, as infantry tanks, were no match for the heavier German Panthers and Mark IVs armed with 75 mm guns. Several of these were now reported to be entrenched in front.

Unlike the other companies which had run into opposition, we made our way in comparative safety through cultivated fields and orchards round the right flank. Unknown to us the other companies were now heavily engaged. The sun beat strongly on our helmets as we walked unmolested along tracks piled high with tomato boxes, passing occasional dead pigs and cows killed by shellfire, their legs stiffening at obscene angles and their stomachs extended like balloons. Seeing the leading file of men sheering away in turn from one alarming sight at the bottom of a ditch, I walked over to find out what it was. The bodies of six British soldiers and a captain lay spreadeagled where they must have been killed the previous afternoon. I had never seen human corpses before – they looked curiously yellow and drained of their blood which was black and clotted on their tattered battledresses. Already the smell of death had attracted a swarm of flies. The sight was quite repulsive.

The Brigadier appeared from nowhere and gave my company commander a rocket in front of all of us for not advancing straight up a particular road instead of keeping to one side as we had done. I could not see what was wrong with that. The road then branched and our advance ran through further tobacco plantations with my platoon now in the lead. Suddenly there was a crack of bullets like whiplashes round my ears. Together with the rest of my leading section I leapt into a ditch and tried to detect from which tobacco field the firing came. I then ordered the leading section, in best battle-school style, to give covering fire while I assaulted round the flank with my other two sections. Anticlimax! There was not a soul there; only some muddy footmarks indicating that this German outpost had withdrawn. I was beginning to feel that war was not quite so glorious as the history books described. For here people managed to get killed without ever seeing the enemy.

Right Flank now had to cross a railway line near its first objective, a disused tobacco factory beside the strategic crossroads in front and to the west of Battipaglia. It was apparently now used for canning and lay beyond an abandoned barracks and the local railway station. I found a small tunnel on my map and crawled under the railway line, followed by my own platoon and Bobby, my company commander. While talking to him I suddenly saw Germans strolling about unconcernedly alongside the tobacco factory about a hundred yards away. They were carrying Spandau machine-guns and looked rather sinister in their coal-scuttle helmets. I trained my binoculars on them and examined, like a deer stalker, the quarry we had been trained to kill. Some wearing slouch caps looked quite ordinary individuals and were chatting away to each other, oblivious of our presence. I grabbed one of my platoon's three Bren machine-guns and carefully trained the tip of its foresight onto the nearest group. One slight pressure of the forefinger and I could have killed several of my fellow men and sent the others scattering. But Bobby ordered me not to shoot as we were now well advance of the Battalion and were required to maintain our present position, as an observation post, under the Germans' noses. The other platoons of the company were now entrenched in the orchard behind.

Meanwhile other platoons had been helping another company of the Battalion to clear the disused Italian barracks on our left, which they did after quite a skirmish in the course of which one platoon officer was caught under fire on the enormous surrounding wire fence and had to be rescued by his platoon sergeant, Sergeant Lumsden, MM. This other company had apparently had a rough time of it. Their advance had led them into range of the German tanks and machine-guns and they had suffered a number of killed and wounded. Our intrepid Church of Scotland padre was hit by machine-gun fire trying to help the wounded. Worst of all a shell from an 88mm gun then landed right on top of battalion headquarters, just missing Colonel Guy, killing our Adjutant, and seriously wounding one of our best company commanders from desert days.

Meanwhile my position in the forward observation post remained comparatively peaceful as we had not yet been spotted. We watched Germans coming and going all day round the tobacco factory in front and we mortared them thoroughly with the aid of a spotter from the Battalion's 3-inch mortar team. Unfortunately we could not range on the nearest Germans who were much too close; but we must have caused casualties to those further away.

That night my platoon maintained a standing patrol to the east of the tobacco factory where we were consumed by mosquitoes which frequent this malarial plain; we had to remain on the *qui vive* for an expected counter-attack – which did not however materialise. By next morning we were beginning to feel our lack of sleep.

Throughout the following day our platoon officers and the second-in-command took turn about manning the observation post. In between we returned to our slit trenches in the orchard some 300 yards to the rear. Here the trees were laden with ripe grapes, pears and peaches. The Germans were now shelling us and our own artillery (just landed) dropped a few shells short. It was obvious too that we were now up against the main German defensive line, for German Spandau machine-guns were firing incessantly over our heads from the tobacco factory itself but without appearing to fire at any particular target. Dug-in tanks also machine-gunned the area and occasionally fired armour-piercing shells through the trees. These did little damage beyond bringing down showers of apples and saving us the trouble of climbing to pick them.

The whole area was reported to be filling rapidly with German reinforcements as it was now two days since our landing and we had only progressed inland for about four miles. To our immediate west Montecorvino airfield had just been captured but later became impossible to maintain as it came under shell and machine-gun fire.

From the wireless it now appeared that the Germans had regained control of the whole of Italy and that no Italian units had come over to our side. Indeed one would not have expected any self-respecting Italians to do so. Opposite our two British infantry divisions at Salerno the 16th Panzer Division was now reinforced by four other German divisions. Although we did not know such details at the time, we realised that the situation around and to the west of Battipaglia was getting serious and, in particular, in front of the fruit-laden orchard where we were entrenched.

Now that the Germans had held the first impact of our advance they started counter-attacking in the afternoon all along the front. They drove the Royal Fusiliers and beyond them the Americans out of Battipaglia. It looked as if the Germans might even overrun a company of Grenadiers only hundreds of yards to our right where there was quite a gap into which they appeared to have infiltrated.

In this critical situation rumour now became rife. Some said the Second Front had started in France, others that the Salerno beachhead was about to be withdrawn; others that the 8th Army advancing from the south was about to relieve us. None of these rumours was strictly true, although the question of the withdrawal of the beachhead was apparently considered with the Commander-in-Chief flying in to assess the situation. As for myself, I wanted nothing more than a long quiet sleep; what with the danger and incessant noise of battle about one's ears, sleep had been impossible during the daytime. The previous night had been spent on standing patrol; the night before advancing to take over the other battalion's positions; and the night before that on the landing craft which itself was hardly conducive to slumber. I had not yet acquired the old soldier's habit of snatching every spare hour of daylight for sleep – so necessary if mind and body are to stand up to the nervous strain of front-line fighting.

I was still feeling like sleep on my afternoon watch, despite the close proximity of the enemy. Suddenly, however, all thoughts of rest vanished on seeing an unusual number of German soldiers in the fields to my immediate front. I examined them through my binoculars and saw with relief they were not actually attacking us but merely moving up into forward positions. They came walking across the field in file and halted less than a hundred yards from my place of concealment and in direct line to my left along the railway embankment. They obviously did not know we were so near. Then from behind the embankment, where there was a field of maize, someone shouted something and the reply, in German, came from a voice on my own side. In momentary panic I feared we were surrounded and caught like rats in a trap till I remembered the Germans did not know of our presence. I posted one of my men to protect our escape tunnel back under the railway line, and sent information to company Headquarters of the German movements with the expressed hope that the observation post could now be withdrawn before we were overrun.

Ten minutes later a message came back that the observation post was to be withdrawn immediately and I was to report at once to Company Headquarters for an order group. As I passed through the other platoon positions on the way, I noticed that the older guardsmen had several chickens roasting over camp fires. I wonder who ate them in the end.

At headquarters Bobby, my company commander, had just arrived from battalion headquarters with orders, not for withdrawal, but for a repeat attack by the Battalion in an hour's time on the tobacco factory itself and the vital crossroads beyond. Our company's start line was to be the railway embankment which I had just seen occupied by Germans. When I inquired if battalion headquarters had absorbed my recent information, Bobby said he didn't know but that senior authority considered the vital crossroads beyond the tobacco factory must be captured at all costs. Certainly with the close nature of the country and the amount of tanks the Germans had, this appeared to be the key to their ability to counter-attack. Nevertheless, owing to the critical situation on our right, Bobby said he fully expected the whole attack to be called off at the last moment.

Into our midst there now rushed a tattered individual from the battalion on our right who said his platoon had just been overrun. I don't think it had, but some Germans did seem to have infiltrated behind us as a Spandau, with its unmistakable rapidity, started firing from an orange grove to our rear. Or was it perhaps a captured Spandau being used by our own side? Nobody seemed to know exactly what was happening. In the gathering darkness we studied our maps by torchlight and then endeavoured to instruct our platoons regarding the attack, which my platoon was to lead. I knew, of course, about the access tunnel underneath the railway line which would avoid us having to ascend the embankment and cross the railway where we would be enfiladed by Spandau fire.

I had just time to give hurried orders when our supporting artillery barrage commenced. It was intense and accurate such as only our seasoned ex-8th Army gunners could fire; but the situation could not have looked worse. Even if successful, it was difficult to see how we could remain on such an objective right in front of the rest of the Allied Line. Nor would we have tank support to combat any German tanks that tried to counter-attack. 'F' Company were to attack on the left of the main road while 'G' Company were to advance up the road from the railway station to re-occupy the vital tobacco factory itself.

Night had now fallen although there was bright moonlight. The thunderous roar of our own guns and distant explosions from those of the enemy, followed by the interlacing whine as the shells crossed overhead, formed a deafening accompaniment – so deafening that one soon lost all sense of sound. We seemed to be groping our way silently through the moonlight as in a dream. We kept right up under our own barrage, for I knew it was better to risk casualties from one's own shrapnel than to let the enemy have a few seconds breathing space to recover themselves after the barrage lifted. Owing to the height of the railway embankment we were able to keep to within fifty yards of our shells bursting on the far side, thereby achieving unusual covering fire. Two of my men, however, were hit by one shell falling short.

I thought we might have to fight to secure the tunnel itself carrying a small river under the railway line for it was here I had seen the Germans forming up. But there was no interference as I got Sergeant Stewart's men down into the knee-deep stream as silently as possible and formed up the remainder behind. We had timed things to a nicety, for our barrage now lifted, dying away into the distance and leaving us only with the sound of water dripping from our sodden clothes.

We clambered catlike out of the far end of the tunnel where the open fields – white in the moonlight and flanked by the even more ghostlike tobacco factory – stretched across to the Battipaglia road. We spoke in whispers and as we formed in extended line our pace was stealthy and feline. A long dark hedge which stretched across the fields to the main road seemed the only vestige of cover, while on our left the railway embankment in deep shadow stretched as far as the railway station. It was here that I had seen the Germans forming up. But now there was no sound except for the subdued chirping of crickets. Sergeant Stewart whispered that he thought there was a booby-trap on the path. I advanced, revolver in hand, to examine it and found a rifle leaning against a carrier of mortar bombs. For a second it did not dawn on me these must be German. Then suddenly, and almost subconsciously, I noticed a cluster of black figures lying sheltering along the embankment at my very elbow. I spun round, yelling 'Hands up!' in German. There was a shower of sparks as one of them fired at me. I promptly fired my revolver point-blank at the nearest two who were now sitting up; and they rolled towards me screaming. As a practised revolver shot and at that range, I could hardly miss. All hell now broke loose as the silence was shattered. Everyone started yelling. Other Germans, sitting on the embankment, fired at us. Ex-Sergeant Hutchison finished one of them off, then, thank God, the remainder stuck up their hands.

An awful savagery now seemed to take hold of us as we rushed along the embankment shouting oaths and shooting at Germans who were lying there. I felt as if some wild animal had got me by the throat and I had to keep shouting and shooting or else my normal self would return bringing fear along with it. There was even a savage pleasure in it. One German was truculent, refusing to double back down the line, and while we were arguing and threatening him, other Germans fired at us out of a trench thirty yards off. I shot him point-blank; the effect was electric and we rushed headlong at the Spandau. Oblivious to sound again, one only saw the flashes coming from the gun muzzles and the sparks from our own rifles as we closed in, firing from the hip. I fired the remaining shots from my revolver. Paterson was going berserk with rifle and bayonet.

We doubled along a hedge which led to our objective, the main road, giving tongue like a pack of wolves. I found it awkward reloading my revolver on the move; in addition my belt was failing miserably to keep up my soaking trousers. I had completely abandoned all thought of tactics and had allowed the lust of battle to take hold. We were halfway alongside of the tobacco factory when some enemy entrenched there opened fire on us, but in the dark their bullets passed over our heads. As we were now right in the middle of their positions they obviously did not know where to shoot. One German came running up shouting and we shot at him amidst much cursing. It was incredible how much we all cursed and swore.

My leading section overran another Spandau post without a shot, but on reaching the main road to Battipaglia, which was our objective, we were heavily fired on from positions guarding a bridge. This was protected by a four-foot ditch and impossible for my first section, now reduced to four men, to assault alone. As another guardsman dropped wounded, I yelled at the second section to come up. They seemed to take a long time and their sergeant was a new man who was in a daze. Some of the Germans were now standing up to shoot at us as we crouched by the hedge shooting back. I fired another drumful from my revolver to try and make them keep their heads down. When the second section came level we all assaulted together, clambering over the ditch. In the darkness one was only conscious again of the sparks coming from the enemy's gun muzzles. One German threw a grenade which landed in the ditch at my feet, while Hutchison who had been foremost in the attack got a burst of Spandau through his shoulder. After some wild shooting the rest of this German post surrendered and we clambered over a fence on to the main Battipaglia road. We were now at the back of the tobacco factory. I sent a man back with Hutchison who seemed badly wounded. He was one of the old desert sergeants who had been demoted for his part in the North African 'mutiny'.

I was now so flushed with excitement that I was finding it difficult to think clearly or to control my guardsmen who were rampaging round like foxhounds. Sergeant Stewart, still surviving but with only two left in his section, insisted on trying to attack a German platoon in a spinney to our right and kept yelling at them in broad Scots, 'Come on out and fight you f...... bastards!' The Germans, however, would not oblige and did not even shoot as there was such a mix-up now of British and Germans. I yelled at Stewart to come back so that we could get organised for consolidating on our objective. One tiny little German who looked absurd in an outsized coal-scuttle helmet kept on wanting to surrender to us but leapt back into his trench whenever there was another burst of fire. Finally he came running across the road to join us amidst roars of applause.

Guardsman Chadwick, who was now temporarily commanding

my second section, was trying to locate some Spandaus firing on us from the direction of the crossroads and got a bullet through his mess tin for his pains. He was an old soldier, at one time in the Special Air Service. I thought they might be British Bren guns and not Spandaus firing, so I shouted the password 'Wellington' in their direction. But there was no reply of 'Barracks', only dead silence. As they stopped shooting, however, they must have imagined I was a German. I had thought they might have been 'G' Company who should have been level by this time. (Later I was to learn that 'G' Company managed to fight their way into the disused factory building, but later had to be withdrawn for fear of being cut off.) 'F' Company, to their left, who had already lost their company commander, fared even worse. The first wave of their attack had been shot to pieces in the bright moonlight and two of their platoon officers killed. The Germans had then counter-attacked and overrun the rest of the company. Their Company Sergeant-Major, an old Battalion man, escaped later in the night only to be killed by a shell on rejoining our lines.

My company had only reached its objective because we had been able to use the tunnel under the embankment to move right in under our barrage before the Germans had time to recover. Also because there was such a mix-up in the darkness that the Germans did not know who was who and where to shoot. Meanwhile, oblivious of the fact that we were the only company to capture its objective, we strutted about as proud as peacocks in the midst of a still intact German battalion heavily supported by tanks.

8 Platoon now crossed the road on to the fields beyond and started to try and dig in; but the ground was as hard as concrete and they only had small entrenching tools. As the moon rose I sent Chadwick's section in the direction of the crossroads, which was now a hundred yards to our left, wishing to know if the shouting and noise of tracked vehicles coming from that direction meant the arrival of 'G' Company. Suddenly Chadwick shouted to look out as there were tanks coming straight down the road at us. I didn't react at once, thinking these might be our own Shermans. There was a sinister grinding and squeaking of bogie wheels and two German tanks or half-tracks came clattering straight for us down the tarmac. The road was a death trap with high barbed wire fences on either side and our Piat (anti-tank projector) was with platoon headquarters. Cursing the moonlight, I yelled at everyone to lie face downwards at the side of the road, trusting the tank driver's lack of vision. I could feel all my

muscles contracting with fear as the metal tracks passed within yards of my elbow scattering sparks in all directions. The tanks, however, passed straight on over the bridge beside 7 Platoon.

I stood up again, sobered and bewildered, not knowing of any battle drill to fit such a perilous situation and trying desperately to think what to do next. I thought that if the reserve company would now come up, we might still have taken the tobacco factory and vital crossroads; but things were now beginning to get out of hand. I told my leading section to get quickly into a house (which, unknown to me, was full of Germans) and ran back to try to find my platoon HQ with its anti-tank projector which had been lost in the mêlée. I only got as far as my second section when I saw some more tanks approaching from the other direction with the moonlight glinting on their turrets. To my horror I realised that they were not simply motoring through us again but were part of a coordinated infantry-supported counter-attack. Long lines of German infantry stretched behind them, coming in from our right side and rear. They quickly overran my platoon HQ who were now climbing on to the road, finding there was little they could do against a combination of enemy infantry and armour when they were not dug in. Company headquarters, which was also coming up, only just managed to shoot their way out.

The tables were now completely turned and the rest was a humiliating fiasco. I got caught on a barbed wire fence under the very guns of the tanks but managed to extricate myself, shouting to all my nearby men to follow me into the ditch. I arrived there with four others. We were hardly into the ditch before the converging lines of German infantry started jumping over it and some took up positions further along. The five of us started a somewhat futile discussion on how to rectify the situation as more half-tracks came coursing down the road to stop opposite with a screech of brakes and seal us off from Ian Fraser's platoon which had crossed on to the other side of the main road wondering what was happening. I heard Chadwick shouting for me and then silence which meant that he too had been put 'in the bag'. We poked a gun gingerly over the top of the bank, but firing it would have served no purpose as there were now Germans behind and in front of us and our prisoners mixed up with them. On all sides Germans were crawling out of slit trenches which we had failed to clear or perhaps even see in our initial assault.

Some Germans now came clearing down the ditch along which we had started to crawl. They must have seen us jump into it for they searched methodically and extracted two of my party at gunpoint. But they missed Coyle, Murphy and myself. We were lying full length in the muddy water under some bramble bushes so they never saw us and passed further on down the ditch. We started to crawl again. The ditch became deep and dark and completely overgrown with brambles. It was very quiet down below – apart from the droning of the mosquitoes. I stalked what I thought to be a wounded German in our path with my revolver, but it turned out to be a piece of sacking.

Germans were passing frequently along the path overhead, talking noisily. I tried to make out what they were saying, as I knew some German – but I could only catch the word 'Engländer'. I suppose they were re-occupying the ground we had captured and recovering their dead and wounded. It was an unpleasant feeling to be suddenly a fugitive instead of an attacker. The three of us crawled another fifty yards until the ditch became full of water and the brambles grew right down to the surface. We seemed to make an awful noise splashing. I returned my revolver to its holster as I did not think it would fire any more after being stuck in the mud. The mortification of the situation weighed heavily upon me, especially the knowledge that the Germans must have captured all our wounded and retaken a number of their own prisoners. I did not relish returning to the Battalion with only two of my men.

A large shell crater blocked the ditch and I could hear Germans talking on the other side where they had re-occupied a machine-gun post. It was obvious we would have to stay in this ditch till the moon sank in the early morning and the dawn mists allowed a chance to crawl across the open fields to the railway line. It was now about 10 p.m. and the moon's vertical rays glinted on the water of the ditch which submerged us up to our waists. I found difficulty in getting one leg under a bush as a party of Germans passed overhead conversing in loud voices. I thought one of them had seen me, as he appeared to stop, but he passed on again. We had not yet abandoned hope: there still seemed a chance that if the other companies had been successful, the reserve company might be sent through to regain our sector. At one moment indeed I thought I heard guttural Scots voices shouting 'Come here' – but it was only some Germans. It now became evident that the attack had been called off as a costly failure, although it may have helped to knock the Germans off balance at a time when they themselves had been preparing to counter-attack and drive us back on to the beaches.

The ensuing two hours were like a nightmare, but more unreal. So complete was my exhaustion, I was too tired to care. I did not even feel the discomfort of the water in which I lay, or of a gash on my leg. Although there was a German post within twenty yards I dozed off for half an hour. Murphy did the same, but we later had to wake him because of his snores. He then started a feverish coughing that I feared must reveal our presence. Suddenly some Verey lights went up beyond the main road on the original company objective, and there was a roar from about six machine-guns firing belt after belt, all at once. Our spirits revived at the prospect of rescue. But there followed dead silence. It was only some remnants of the company surrounded by the Germans behind their lines. This turned out to be Ian Fraser's platoon which had followed behind us through the gap we had opened up.

It was now about 11 p.m. We were getting very cold sitting in the water, but had to do so as Germans were still passing to and fro above our heads. Murphy's coughing was now becoming uncontrollable despite a handkerchief we stuffed in his mouth. It was incredible that the Germans did not hear us. I decided that we would have to start crawling away from them towards the main road again and wait there for the moon to set before making a dash for it. But our movements led to unavoidable splashing and brought on a further spasm of hysterical coughing from Murphy. The Germans really did hear us this time. They started shouting to each other and came running towards us. I now realised the game was up when they were standing right above covering us with their Schmeisser machine-pistols.

3

The Other Side of the Hill

I must confess that my first feelings on capture were not of shame but of immense relief at being still alive. The Germans appeared upset by our presence so near their positions and rushed our efforts at extrication from the ditch, pulling my revolver from its holster and throwing it on the ground as if it were a scorpion. Then they grew more easy and reassured. I said jokingly in my indifferent German that they had taken a long time to find us, when we had been only a few yards away for nearly two hours. They behaved correctly and did not even submit us to the degradation of walking with our hands above our heads. In fact I strolled back to the crossroads chatting to a German sergeant who seemed quite pleasant. I now saw the German positions around the tobacco factory itself, formerly bypassed by us, and could not comprehend why they had not enfiladed us more effectively. Each was well-prepared, reinforced with railway sleepers and contained businesslike-looking Krauts in grey overcoats and steel helmets. They had clearly outnumbered us.

We were now put on to half-tracks at the crossroads where several German tanks were also parked. Here I met some men of the other platoon with their wounded and Ian Fraser, their new platoon officer, who had only assumed command half an hour before the attack. We dropped the wounded off down the road at a German first aid post. Our company piper had a bad wound and seemed pretty far gone. Here were more lines of German Mark IV tanks, parked nose to tail; and obviously waiting in readiness for the pending German counter-attack.

One had to confess to a certain sense of relief at being now on the safer side of the battle line, seeing all this German armour lined up ready for attack. Ian and I sat at the front of a half-track beside the driver while other Germans and some of our men were piled in behind. We exchanged biscuits and cigarettes and a kindly German put a field-dressing on the gash on my thigh. There was a certain false heartiness about it all, like a celebration between the victorious and losing teams after an international football match. As losers go, we even seemed reasonably popular opponents for these men of a German Panzer division. I asked one of them what he thought of his Italian allies and he spat and said, 'Schweinen!' When they in turn started to become curious about the number and quality of American troops on our right flank, I replied, 'Das kann ich nicht sagen' ('That I cannot say'), which appeared to cause amusement and was repeated with laughter round the other Germans on the carrier.

The vehicle now stopped while a German NCO talked to his officer. There were many more tanks in this area, parked along the road with little apparent regard for concealment from the air. I think I could have made a run for it at this point while some of the men were urinating. The chances of being shot under such circumstances seemed negligible compared with the dangers we had undergone in the recent attack. But just for the moment I felt too utterly exhausted to care much about anything except sleep.

The vehicle started again and proceeded for about three miles until it finally stopped outside a building used as German billets. Here we disembarked and were taken to a lawn behind a house where we were left to sleep on the grass in a shivering group surrounded by several armed guards. Escape was clearly impossible from this position. Clothed only in soaking wet khaki drill, I still managed to sleep fitfully, so utterly tired out did I feel. Whenever I awoke I could see the baleful glow of the guards' fag-ends as they smoked in the darkness. They looked liked wolves' eyes on perpetual watch.

Dawn came at last and the Germans brought us a canteen of cold ersatz coffee. Later they brought us some more which was warm and not too bad. Luckily some of the men of Ian's platoon still had their small packs containing rations which they shared round for breakfast. We even managed a brew of tea. It was also gratifying that they still maintained discipline under Ian and myself.

As the sun rose all the church bells started ringing from the hilltop villages to summon the peasants to early Mass for it was Sunday. In contrast, around our place of confinement the German tank crews, suntanned and stripped to the waist, were assiduously cleaning their guns and maintaining their motor transport. I could not help admiring their keenness and physique, it being easy to forget that all this youthful energy was now directed towards killing one's fellow countrymen. There was no lounging in corners. They wore khaki drill shorts like ourselves but, unlike us, khaki caps with long peaks. Also unlike us, the officers and men all saluted each other whenever they joined another group which was never our practice in the front line as opposed to on formal parade.

To pass the time I chatted in doggerel German to a genial guard with a pleasant face who turned out to be an ex-ski-instructor from Austria, where, so he said, he used to meet many English whom he liked. I asked him what German soldiers thought of our soldiers and he replied, 'Brave, but stupid.' His division had not fought us before and he told me they had just come south from fighting the Russians at Rostov. I asked him what the fighting had been like on the Eastern Front and he said it all depended on whether you could get good billets in the winter. In Poland the inhabitants' houses had been just passable but those of the Russian peasants were beyond description and mostly unfit for habitation. He conceded, however, that they were fanatical soldiers. He asked if I would like to see some Russian soldiers captured at Stalingrad. His 16th Panzer Division apparently used these ex-Soviet soldiers as mess orderlies like we used Italian prisoners in North Africa. One of them was brought forward to speak to me. He had a roguish smiling face with Slav features but could speak little German. He said he came from Kubishev. I asked him why he was now wearing German uniform after taking part in the heroic defence of Stalingrad. He merely laughed and replied, 'Good food, good pay!' He was obviously a bit of a comic and the Germans ragged him playfully as if he were a tame dog.

As my guard talked freely I was anxious to know whether the tenacity of the German opposition in this area meant they had known we were coming. He knew little, except that his division had been ordered to stand by and had even been on manoeuvres the night before we landed that almost coincided with our own. It was evident that although they did not know the exact time and place of our landings, the 'alert' order had been given, thus enabling large forces to be rushed to support the defence when our initial invasion had been checked. They now had no doubt of their ability to drive us back off the narrow bridgehead.

I had to remember that talking like this with one's captors was contrary to King's Regulations. But my Austrian guard was a mere private and there was no question of his interrogating me. Eventually his officer curtly ended our conversation and told him to stand back and stop talking to the 'Englander'. His sergeant, however, was a decent fellow and allowed me to collect some figs off a nearby tree for my men.

We had now been lying down for several hours in the sunshine which was the first time for several days we had been able truly to relax. There was no sound of battle and comparatively little risk unless one made the purely personal choice of trying to escape. When I felt more recovered I thought I might consider doing so. But not just yet unless a golden opportunity presented itself. For it would be much more difficult once one was locked up in a prison camp.

A young captain came up and asked me to move my men into the shadows beside some tanks and other vehicles. I did not know whether this was to get us out of the blazing sun or under his more direct surveillance; but he seemed quite pleasant about it. The only one of these Germans whom I disliked so far was the lieutenant who had stopped me talking. He was a vicious-looking man with small side-whiskers who chain-smoked black cheroots. In the course of the morning I had to translate this unpleasant lieutenant's orders to three of our men to dig a long line of graves in front of where we were sitting. When the line began to approximate to the number of our party, I was struck with a sudden fear that this was intended to be our own last resting place. One had, after all, heard bloodcurdling accounts of German atrocities. Surely at least the captain, or our young Austrian guard, would not let us all be shot like this in cold blood. I studied their individual countenances intently but, the lieutenant apart, they still looked quite affable. Yet somehow I could not quite trust them as a national group. I felt that an order to shoot might suddenly be barked out by the lieutenant and that then these ordinary individuals might give effect to the worst aspects of national antagonism.

My temporary fears were groundless. In due course a truckload of German corpses arrived which were then buried by the Germans themselves. They must have been the victims of our last night's attack or of our artillery fire further down the road.

It was becoming irksome, now that I was partly rested, having to take orders from the unpleasant lieutenant and I was beginning to favour availing myself of any opportunity for escape. It was very humiliating, now that one had time to think about it, to have been captured like this in one's first attack. But I had no real complaint, so far, of German treatment. They had not even touched my wrist-watch and had returned my wallet with all the liras in it.

[44]

About midday we were given a snack meal of *knackerbrod* with limitless Danish butter. I took the occasion to fill my pockets with extra packets of biscuits which the German corporal in charge readily handed over. As one of the guardsmen observed, when following suit, he was a 'guid wee lad'.

The captain now requested me to form up our men for marching off. We were apparently to go to Divisional Headquarters for interrogation. I told the guardsmen to give the Germans a bit of 'bull' which they did magnificently in best Buckingham Palace style. There was an officers' conference in progress in the middle of a group of Volkswagen vehicles. They all wore shorts and long peaked caps and saluted as they joined or left the group; everyone seemed in high spirits. They were studying maps spread out on the bonnet of one of the vehicles but stopped to look at us as we formed up in style before marching off. Our column of about fifteen men was given only one German guard armed with a Schmeisser automatic which seemed very lax. The only difficulty was that we were in the German headquarters area with a lot of troops and tanks about. Also it might not be so easy to get back inside the battle perimeter at a time when there was some possibility of the whole bridgehead being withdrawn.

Ian Fraser and I marched at the head of the column beside our single diminutive German guard. The road was halfway up the mountains which back the Salerno Plain and was partly concealed from the ground below by olive groves. We passed a tank park where the barrels of the tank guns were being pulled through by their crews. Other tanks were moving along the road and we could also hear more of them rumbling along a parallel road higher up the hillside. The 16th Panzer Division looked as if it was marshalling for attack.

Our road now led out into an open space – no longer concealed by olive groves – and where the precision of our marching must have attracted the attention of some long-range gunnery officer or perhaps even a British warship in the bay. There was suddenly a deep boom from that direction followed several seconds later by the whine of an approaching shell and then a terrific explosion on the road in front. It just missed a Volkswagen vehicle which had come round the corner and which now shot off in the opposite direction. The top of the vehicle was camouflaged with branches, giving its occupants the appearance of two very scared birds in a nest. We scattered into the ditch as a complete salvo now descended on us. The German guard lying beside me kept banging my heel with his gun barrel to make me move further down the ditch; he appeared to be absolutely terrified. Then everyone started running up the road again as more shells landed. It was all rather comical. I found myself running behind the German guard at one point; he kept shouting and seemed uncertain whether to shoot or not.

I joined Ian up the ditch and we now decided to make off while our inadequate guard was marshalling the other prisoners. Unfortunately another German Volkswagen appeared round the corner at this crucial moment; so we had to smile at the occupants and pretend to be sheltering from the shellfire. They slowed down as they came level with us and looked at us suspiciously, but then continued on their way. So we made off up the hill behind. It had all been too ridiculously easy, as I suppose it usually is before one is firmly locked up in a prison camp.

Our plan was to move away from our lines to draw the Germans onto a false scent; and then make our way back to Salerno from the west along the mountains at the head of the valley. We did not run – it would have been obvious to all the numerous Germans in the vicinity – but walked very deliberately across the road towards the mountains at the head of the valley. We looked sufficiently like Germans in our khaki drill uniforms and so we just ambled along talking to each other. However, we slowly increased our speed in the knowledge that troops and half-tracks would soon be on our tail from Divisional Headquarters where the others had been taken.

After walking about a mile we decided to lie doggo among some thick sedges where we were totally invisible at three yards' range. After the initial exhilaration of escape I now felt so overcome with fatigue that I dozed off into a deep slumber.

I woke with a start as the sun was declining and the mosquitoes were beginning to feast on my bare legs. I could not stop moving and scratching because of the mosquitoes and had unfortunately cut off my trouser legs earlier on as they had been badly torn on the barbed wire fence the night before. Ian, who had been concealed a short distance away in case of surprise, was whispering to me furiously to stop scratching. There were some Germans just beside us; he had heard them talking only fifty yards away and could not move to stop me for fear of making more noise himself. I hadn't heard a thing.

I still could not settle down. After waiting another hour and making sure the coast was clear, we decided to move on. It was now about six o'clock. We looked for some concealed route, but nothing presented itself; so we decided to repeat our successful ruse of walking out in the open like Germans. We had to pass beside one of the main German tank parks with lines of tanks whose crews paid us no attention whatsoever as we passed them deliberately talking to each other. Certainly we must have looked sufficiently like them because when, later on, we approached a small farmstead, the Italian peasants came running out and stood in a row against the wall with their hands up shouting 'Kamerad'. Their thin bearded faces bore the pathetic look of animals about to be whipped and knowing there is no escape. They seemed absolutely petrified. When we finally managed to assure them we were not 'Tedeschi' but 'Inglesi' their welcome knew no bounds and they rushed on us whimpering with pleasure. We were embraced by each old bearded man in turn while the womenfolk wept profusely and fingered our clothes. I suppose it was merely that we symbolised the end of the war for them and they thought Ian and I were the spearhead of the liberators. As we were clearly hungry they also fed us on the best food they could find – goat's milk cheese, raw eggs, figs and Italian bread, kept stale and soaked for eating. We parted from them as night was falling and were directed towards the little village of Olevano Salita, higher up the mountain.

After climbing for about two miles we passed a cowshed where white oxen snorted and shuffled through their evening meal of hay. Without being observed, we ate figs which the farmer had laid out to dry on trestle tables and then disposed ourselves for sleep by push-ing our legs into a haystack, taking it in turns to keep watch. But I couldn't sleep like this and, in any event, had already slept that forenoon. When it became Ian's turn to snore away, I was tortured by the inadvisability of staying here till daybreak without having yet crossed the German-patrolled road to Avellino which was still above us. I could hear German convoys moving along it with the rumble of occasional tanks. About 2 a.m. therefore, I woke Ian and suggested we move on.

A rough track led upwards towards the village which straddled the road. The moon had risen now and shone brilliantly through the silhouettes of the olive trees as we climbed up the terraces just below Olevano. A runnel of clear mountain water filled a stone basin where we washed our faces and felt for the soft bunches of grapes among the tendrils of the vines and for the figs in the leafy darkness of their branches. The thick gnarled trunks of the olives showed that they must have been centuries old.

The quiet was suddenly shattered by a German motor-cycle patrol entering the village just above. We ran across the road and started to climb up the olive terraces on the other side. This set a lone watchdog howling, soon to be joined in wailing chorus by every dog in the vicinity. We heard people shouting and at once imagined the Germans were on our trail. Taking off our boots to make less noise, we ran furiously up the precipitous face of the hill till we lay in the arbutus scrub overlooking the village. Everything was now silent again except for the pounding of our hearts. The village shone out brilliantly below in the moonlight. Out beyond and hundreds of feet below lay the Plain and Bay of Salerno – a sea of silver mist lit by occasional flashes of gunfire. We could also hear the thumping of guns on the beaches and around Battipaglia where our brigade must still have been battling; bright flashes could be seen lighting the surface of the mist.

Up on the mountains it was now bitterly cold and we tried to sleep back to back to gain some semblance of warmth. Sometimes we ran up and down to restore the circulation. A saving grace, however, was the absence of mosquitoes which had infested the plain.

When dawn broke a blanket of mist still covered the battlefield below from where the muffled sounds of gunfire drifted upwards. It sounded almost as if the rumblings of war came from some subterranean battleground. Patches of sea were visible through breaks in a smokescreen which must have been laid by our ships to confuse the German gunners. We learned later that this day and the next were the most critical for the beachhead as the Germans were shelling its whole length and counter-attacking in force.

After making sure that Olevano below us was temporarily clear of Germans, we descended the mountain to try to get some food and water as we had finished the last of our German *knackerbrod*. I also wanted a dressing for the gash on my thigh. As we entered the village some Italian women, seeing we were fair-haired, mistook us for Germans and deliberately pretended not to hear our requests for water. But eventually making ourselves plain in English, we were hustled into a house in the main street which happened to belong to the mayor. Conversation was difficult as neither of us spoke Italian; but an old priest, with whom Ian was able to communicate in Latin, acted as interpreter. When we had finally reassured the village elders who crowded into the room behind us that we had not been seen by the Germans, they fed us and enabled us to wash. I was desperate for a new pair of trousers to keep off the mosquitoes; but here Ian's classical scholarship let him down as it appeared that Balbus had only worn a toga. So I was offered a bath towel. Then one Italian said he would conduct us to caves in a gorge behind the village where some disbanded Italian soldiers were hiding and with whom we could lie up for a few days until the Germans stopped searching for us. This seemed an excellent plan, but as soon as the front door was opened the entire village appeared thronging the street and shouting 'Viva Inglese', thinking they had been liberated!

Our new guide managed to persuade the grown-ups we were only escaped English prisoners and they should therefore return to their homes. But he could not free us from a horde of delighted children who followed us up the mountainside, only dropping off one by one as the path became too precipitous.

The rocky track led for about a mile over a shoulder of the mountain above the Salerno Plain till we came to a gorge with a river running so far below that we could only faintly hear the noise of its rushing water. On the alpine pinnacles towering above our heads faint specks could be seen against the sky. These we were told were Italian soldiers acting as sentinels who whistled across the gorge to each other on our approach. The swarthy Neapolitan women, of Spanish appearance in their gay-coloured shawls, moved to and fro along the goat tracks with baskets on their heads. A human murmur arose above the noise of the river, from the entrance to numerous caves, from under overhanging rocks and from hundreds of bivouacs – for here most of the inhabitants of Battipaglia had apparently taken refuge from the recent Allied bombing which had razed most of their town to rubble. Many of them sat delousing their children in front of the cave entrances. No bombs had fallen as yet in the gorge itself but the refugees still lived in caves just in case. We were told by our guide that the labyrinth in the grotto of San Michele on the cliff face opposite (a former place of pilgrimage) contained over 500 people.

Our guide now led us to another group of caves outside which some Italian soldiers were living under brushwood bivouacs. They gave us food, blankets and ragged clothes which they insisted on us wearing. This was despite our protests that this would place us outside the protection of international law and, if we were caught, might lead to our execution as spies. Their lieutenant, Luigi, who spoke some English, explained that this was also essential to conceal us from the local populace who would be certain to gossip and possibly reveal us to the Germans.

Luigi and his companions came from a Northern artillery regiment and were very conscious of their superiority as Northerners over these Southerners, who they told us were not to be trusted. So they insisted on hiding us in an impenetrable-looking coppice halfway down the mountainside, but sufficiently near the caves for contact and food supply.

In fact many Italians came asking to see the 'Inglese' but were told by our friends that we had continued on our way to Salerno. In their wake came German soldiers. Luigi, whose English was not quite perfect, told us with characteristic charm that the Tedeschi had been 'asking after us'. Next day a German sergeant and some soldiers even searched the first few caves; but our protectors never betrayed us nor wavered in their routine of feeding us twice daily. The meal consisted of one mess tin for two, containing goat's meat, macaroni and pimento. It was all they could get to eat themselves and Ian and I were soon very hungry. One day there was nothing at all. So we went food foraging with the Italians after first climbing down to the river and washing our clothes and ourselves in the ice cold water. Overhanging its stream grew green peaches and walnuts, which we avidly consumed. On the way back an old woman gave us a huge bowl of potatoes in olive oil which we squatted round to consume like natives. I never enjoyed a meal so much.

That night, without telling us their intentions, two of the Italian soldiers, noticing our hunger, walked to Olevano and brought us back a sackful of figs and grapes from under the Germans' noses. They got shot at, too, for their pains.

We grew very fond of Luigi and the other Italians on whose loyalty we had little claim, for they would certainly have been shot by the Germans if found befriending us. There could be no doubt of their courage as individuals. Then there was their humour for life in general and at the war situation in particular; their playful looks one morning as they offered us English cigarettes captured by their regiment at Tobruk, waiting to see if our reaction would be Teutonic and humourless. Then roar upon roar of delighted laughter when they saw we also appreciated the joke. It had to be remembered that the Italians had been our original enemy in Egypt, which they had invaded from Cyrenaica.

There were scores of such Italian soldiers hiding in this gorge who had all formerly been guarding the coastline where we had just landed. Luigi told me that when the Germans had got wind of the pending Italian surrender they had all been disarmed. The Germans then shot twenty of their senior officers, including their General, on the excuse of blackout infringements during an air-raid. All their arms, food and equipment were then removed and they were told to clear out of the Salerno area and make for the North of Italy. Their battalion commander came back remonstrating that he hated the English and wished to continue fighting; but the Germans only stripped him of his uniform and sent him away in his underpants.

According to Marshal Badoglio's broadcast, which we had heard on our landing craft, all Italian forces were now supposed to be fighting on our side, 'working their passage home', as it was called. These Italian troops, however, had no intention of doing so, even if rearmed, and one would not have thought any the better of them if they had.

Although one could no longer see the Salerno battle from this mountain gorge one could, to some extent, gauge its progress from the sounds reverberating around its cave-riddled walls. At first the noise of warfare remained distant while the Germans held our bridgehead and almost forced it into the sea. We also received spasmodic information from our Italians, who in turn obtained their news over the wireless or from refugees moving back from the firing line. It was about this time that the Germans, strongly reinforced with four new divisions in the Battipaglia area, were trying to drive a wedge between the American and British bridgeheads.

After a day or two it became obvious even in our mountain hideout that the situation must have finally turned in our favour. One could now hear the distant roar of Allied artillery along the whole front and best of all the constant drone of our bombers overhead. German aircraft were less and less to be seen flying southwards over our gorge before diving down to strafe the beaches. In the clear September sky we could watch our planes through the interlacing canopy of hazel branches. It seemed as if every bomber in the Mediterranean was now flying over the Gulf of Salerno to rectify the previous situation when there were as many German as British or American aircraft. The noise of their engines overhead was now continuous. We lay all day watching the sunlight flashing on their circling wings and occasionally hearing above the incessant drone the thud of exploding bombs – at first distant as they fell, then shuddering through the gorge till the cliff face took up the echo and roared back its reverberation. We knew that relief could not be far away. Sometimes fighter planes entered the gorge itself, shattering our solitude with the snarl of their engines, all cannons firing in pursuit of a Messerschmitt. It was obvious that we must have regained our airstrip to have such close tactical air support.

Our planes appeared to be bombing everything in sight now that the Luftwaffe was in retreat. One day as we sat on the hilltop at the east end of the gorge some American Lightning fighter-bombers suddenly appeared below us and bombed the beautiful little village of Santa Maria. The next village, Santa Lucia, had housed the German headquarters, but there were no Germans in this one. It was a strange situation to look down from our vantage point on the backs of the circling aircraft; and to watch the mushroom smoke from the bombs billowing upwards to spread a pall over the scene of destruction. It was even stranger to see our Italian companions clapping their hands and shouting, 'Bravo! Bravo!' as one little pink and white house after another disintegrated into rubble. They thought it a magnificent spectacle!

The Allies were now sufficiently sure of themselves to drop a whole battalion of American parachutists behind us on the German lines of communication near Avellino. They were immediately wiped out or taken prisoner, being too far from our advancing troops. Our Italian friends told us they knew about this as two American survivors had just come down our gorge.

The only drawback to the advancing battle line was the closer proximity of German troops. There were now German anti-aircraft guns situated on the rear slope of our mountain and also some Spandau positions at the end of the gorge itself. Hence German soldiers started passing up and down the track beside our hiding place. They used mule or donkey transport for their machine-guns. I was somewhat disconcerted to find that our Italians were still prepared to be seen by and even converse with their erstwhile German comrades. So it was a considerable relief when Luigi and the others finally decided to take to the undergrowth themselves. We all moved further from the track and down a steep scrub-covered slope in the gorge to where a large overhanging rock provided a cave-like shelter. This was to be our final place of refuge and here we slept on beds of dried grass. It was bitterly cold at night as September drew to its close; but in the middle of the day when the sun was up, it was pleasant enough to lie on one's back and listen to the jingling of bells from the herds of goats grazing in the undergrowth; or to turn on one's side and see the sun glinting through the foliage of the hazel bushes on to sheets of pink cyclamen.

We were visited one day by an Italian professor who came from the North and appeared to be a friend of Luigi. He spoke perfect English and had read all Trevelyan's books on Garibaldi and *The Making of Italy*. But by the tone of their conversations I don't think our Italians cared overmuch for the 'Inglesi' whom they had previously been fighting in North Africa. Such is national identity. If they had any inclination towards any of the Allies, it was now clearly towards the Americans who were more likely to give and forgive.

One of our young Italian friends had served as a parachutist in the Italian Army, a battalion of which had formed part of the German parachute force which had successfully captured Crete. He had been awarded a decoration for his part in the landing. He described how he had shut his eyes as he floated down on the New Zealanders while his Italian comrades were shot to shreds in mid-air. I asked him what he thought of Fascism, and he said 'Ah Fascisti! Prima!' and then gave a cock-sparrow demonstration of goose-stepping on military parade before adding morosely, 'Mussolini kaput!' He tried to tell me that I would have liked to be a Fascist myself; at which I expostulated.

Despite our national and political divisions, however, we all got on remarkably well under our overhanging rock in no man's land while Germans, British and Americans slugged it out for possession of Italy – but with the Italians themselves now merely looking on.

Ian and I had so far hardly given thought to getting back within the battle perimeter when it appeated to be automatically moving in our direction. For now at last we could hear the sound of rifle and machine-gun fire from nearby German positions. The bridge at the end of the gorge was even blown and we could hear tanks rumbling along the mountain road behind in full retreat. Soon the firing of Spandaus from the end of our valley became intermittent and the front line appeared to be sufficiently fluid for a chance to return to our own lines.

Next morning the sun shone brilliantly and there was not a cloud in the sky as we made our way along the valley to the Salerno Plain, carefully keeping to the oak woods and taking our Italian friends with us as representatives of the disbanded Italian units in the mountains. They were dressed up for the occasion with tasselled military caps – in contrast to Ian and myself who could not have looked scruffier with our tattered Italian clothes and a week's growth of beard. We walked for a mile or two without seeing a sign of anybody and only hearing one rifle shot. Then, as we emerged from a clearing on to the banks of a river, we were confronted by British Tommies repairing a blown-up bridge. Our Italians wanted to run and embrace them but Ian and I held back, walked up to the bridge as casually as we could and were equally casually greeted by the sappers at work on the girders. 'Blow me down, here's a couple of f...... officer blokes with some f...... Eyeties!' We approached the officer in charge and informed him we were escaped officers from 201 Guards Brigade. He looked dubiously at us as if expecting us to be better turned out and as if to say, 'Who are these damned Eyeties you've got hold of?' Finally, however, having become convinced of our identity, he said, 'Good show,' and drove us in his jeep to a British reconnaissance unit operating nearby. They were just about to continue the advance over the repaired bridge and we gave their Commanding Officer such information as we could about the Germans in front. He was a red-faced hearty fellow and as he marshalled his men looked like a genial master of foxhounds moving off to a fresh draw. He now made available one of his supply trucks to take us back to our own battalion 'B' Echelon near the beaches.

As we drove westwards in our supply truck back to the beaches, our Italians became in uproarious mood and, with the spontaneity of the Latin race, felt the whole occasion to be the greatest of fiestas. Every road seemed full of advancing convoys and every armoured column we swept past they greeted with long-drawn-out cries of 'Bravo' accompanied by claps or cheers. What really appeared to impress them most was the outward panoply of war.

They became more subdued as we approached our own lines for the British were obviously not going to be as friendly as they had first imagined. We were also now running into the battle area where all the oleander trees along the roads were splintered by shellfire and their red and pink blossoms scattered in the dust. Buildings everywhere were demolished or pockmarked by shells. Over all hung the strange and fetid smell of death.

4
Back to the Battalion

Ian and I were given a great welcome at our transport echelon where we arrived in time for lunch. It appeared that the Battalion was now holding a quiet sector of the line just north of Salerno. It was indeed good to be back home.

After lunch we deposited our Italians at Divisional Headquarters with the warmest possible commendations for the way they had befriended us at some peril to themselves. So we bade them a fond and grateful farewell. The staff captain who now interviewed us worked from a luxurious caravan and displayed that condescending attitude to front-line soldiers typical of many staff officers. Ian and I, however, did not have much of interest to convey as the battle line had already moved northwards up the Avellino road. But he was nevertheless willing to tell me what had been happening over the last ten days. He indicated that our abortive attack on the tobacco factory, although ending in defeat, was regarded as having thrown the Germans off balance at a time when they were lining up to counter-attack. He told me the German troops we had been attacking were Panzergrenadiers of the 16th Panzer Division. I was able to tell him that some had been moved down from the Russian Front. Another piece of information was that the heavy battleships in Salerno Bay which had been firing in support were HMS *Warspite* and *Valiant*. One of these may even have fired the shells from its long-range guns which rescued us. One of them, however, had been half sunk by one of the first German flying bombs and had then to limp back to North Africa never to take part in the war again.

The broad picture of the fighting, as now pointed out to me or as subsequently ascertained, was that the road and rail centre at Battipaglia (just to the east of the tobacco factory) had been the key to the battle, for it controlled the main encircling road around the Salerno Plain. Further south the American corps had also advanced inland. Then the trouble really started as new German reinforcements (in addition to the 16th Panzers) poured into the battle area –

including the Hermann Goering, 15th and 29th Panzergrenadiers, and the 26th Panzer Division as well as some paratroops. On the evening of 12 September the Americans were driven out of Battipaglia with heavy losses by a strong German counter-attack headed by forty tanks using flamethrowers. Montecorvino airfield (bravely used by American fighter pilots in support of our forward troops) had become untenable. For a day or two some gallant pilots had tried flying sorties by taking off backwards out to sea and returning to the attack; but this had proved too dangerous and they were withdrawn. Fighter support could therefore only come spasmodically (with long-range fuel tanks) from Sicily. The 46th British Division had taken the town of Salerno after a stiff fight; but for several days the town itself remained in jeopardy, being under constant bombardment.

On 12 September the Americans were driven out of Attavilla and on the 13th out of Albanella, so that at one point their lines were only 1,000 yards from the beaches. But they held on doggedly. Among other new reinforcements was the 82nd Airborne Division intended originally to land on Naples airport where we would have linked up with them; but they were now parachuted into action behind the American front line, so critical was the need there for immediate reinforcements.

On the night of 13/14 September the main German attack had come in on the front of 201 Guards Brigade, intending to break right through to the beaches; but it never penetrated the Coldstream defences, reinforced in the last resort by beach landing parties. Our desert-trained artillery broke up the massed German attack and ended by shooting at German tanks and carriers over open sights. By this time our supporting tanks of the Scots Greys had only six tanks left. It had indeed been the most touch-and-go amphibious landing of the war with at one point the evacuation of the American 5th Army being actively considered.

After our interview at Divisional Headquarters I obtained a lift to the tobacco factory area but sincerely wished I hadn't. My main purpose was to try to identify some of our dead who might have been imperfectly buried there by the Germans. The area now looked strangely small in broad daylight and the fields and vineyards which a few days ago had been so fiercely contested absurdly nondescript. An Italian peasant came up holding his nose and pointed along a ditch. From this unpleasant gesture we understood there were bodies there. We located them by the buzz of flies settled on the earth which lightly covered a wiped-out section of Right Flank. A sergeant's stripes could be seen on an arm protruding above the surface. I helped identify him. Someone said these men had been killed by one of the German tanks firing at them from the road behind when they tried to hold the company's captured objective. The Regimental Sergeant-Major who was with me said he must dig all the others up to see who they were. But I felt nauseated and as they were anyway not from my platoon I felt entitled to return to transport echelon. I passed the body of a dead German swollen with decomposition like a balloon and inadequately covered with an army blanket which someone had thrown over him – a final cloak on the glory of war.

The only solace for this sickening experience was to find my small pack containing my black beret with valuable silver cap star in a bramble bush where I had abandoned it just before capture. I remembered thinking at the time that I might be able to get it back again. It was also good news to learn that of the dozen or so Germans we had taken prisoner as we emerged from the tunnel on the night of our attack two had been officers. A cheering sight too on the road back were a number of German half-tracked vehicles knocked out where they had vainly tried to penetrate the Coldstream defences in their final counter-attack. One looked as if it had even breached our lines at one point.

Back at 'B' Echelon I was able to locate the officers' mess lorry carrying my valise camp bed and all the other belongings I had left behind on landing – or almost all of them. The Quartermaster-Sergeant told me that one of the officers had pirated my map case on the assumption that I was dead. It was with considerable reluctance too that he eventually gave it back. I also received some mail, including a letter from my mother which had been written immediately on hearing of the Italian landings. She wrote that she was delighted that the Army authorities had decided to land me in such a beautiful place as Italy. I was to be certain to visit Florence, especially the Uffizi Gallery, and she also recommended certain hotels to stay in.

That night I slept on my own camp bed in clean pyjamas. The contrasting luxury seemed too good to be true. I slept like a log until about 10 a.m. next morning when the heat of the sun on my face and the noise of lorries moving in and out of the field made further sleep impossible. I shaved, changed into clean battledress and walked over to talk to some friends on the other side of the field. Suddenly all the Oerlikon guns opened up as three German Messerschmitt fighters skimmed over us at treetop level as dumbfounded we watched clusters of bombs descending on us. I dived under the nearest lorry. There was a series of explosions followed by further detonations from a nearby ammunition dump going up in flames and then the cries of our wounded. Our men had been caught napping in the open now that the Luftwaffe had virtually disappeared. Five guardsmen lay dying and another thirteen wounded. Mostly they were pipers or transport drivers from 'B' Echelon. I found the Pipe Major lying groaning on his stomach beside a fence, his shoulders still heaving. I turned him over, only to find a huge cavity behind his ear; so I turned him quickly back again as there was clearly nothing that could be done. Two Battalion clerks had been hit while typewriting in their tent. Greatest loss for me, however, was Ian Fraser, my companion of the last few days, who had a bullet through his chest and thigh. I was lucky to have left my camp bed shortly before the strafing attack as I found it riddled with shrapnel from one bomb explosion.

Next morning 'B' Echelon moved to the security of an orchard above Salerno where 'A' Echelon (containing our fighting vehicles) was already parked. The infantry companies were dug in about a mile away on a rocky ridge to the north. I drove up that evening to report to Colonel Guy, who was very affable and glad to see me back. Bobby Rivers-Bulkeley, my company commander, was now commanding an amalgamated 'F' and 'G' Company as the two companies had each lost half their strength in the recent fighting. The new Adjutant, who had replaced the previous one just killed, asked if I would take over a platoon at once as the Battalion had now lost fifteen officers. But I asked for a day's grace.

This turned out to be a welcome spree with our pioneer officer, Dickie Buckle, to obtain a barrel of wine for the new officers' mess in the town of Salerno. Next day we drove by jeep through the deserted streets of the town and then turned westwards along the corniche coast road where precipitous mountains stretched right down to the shore. At one point where the road passed over a steep gorge on a narrow stone bridge its parapet was being gradually demolished by a German 88 mm gun firing at it from further up the ravine. Every time a vehicle passed over and became momentarily visible to the German gunners one could hear the gun bark; and then just as the vehicle passed behind the protective cliff on the other side – bang! and a shell would hit the parapet. This unpleasant situation had been converted by the local Italians into comic opera. Two *carabinieri*, clothed and armed as for the Napoleonic wars, kept guard at either end and stopped each car. Then they peered round the corner, presumably to see if the German gun was being loaded; with terrific shouts of encouragement and gesticulations each car was then directed over the bridge surrounded by a cheering mob of Italian youths who seemed to think it safer to cross this way rather than by themselves. However, when we crossed with our cheering retinue the gun didn't even fire. Perhaps the Germans thought our jeep too small a target.

We continued along the cliffside road in scenery reminiscent of the Côte d'Azur, with purple mountains overhead and the blue Mediterranean beneath, seen through a vista of pines. We kept on pausing to admire the superlative views and eventually stopped for lunch at Amalfi whose ancient cathedral contains the bones of St Andrew, patron saint of Scotland. A small restaurant yielded some excellent fried squid and potatoes which we washed down with Orvieto. Our hostess, however, turned out to be broad Hackney, having married the Italian proprietor before the war. He took us into his restaurant in the hope that a combination of myself, Dickie and his wife could stop some American GIs breaking his glasses. But the Americans were celebrating. They were Texas Rangers just down from the mountain ridges above, which they had captured in the initial landings. We could see the Stars and Stripes proudly flying from the topmost peaks. Now, armed to the teeth, they lent to this little Italian restaurant the tough guy atmosphere of a Wild West saloon. When we sought a different table, they roared, 'Hey, you goddamned Limeys, come in and join us for a drink', which we duly did.

After lunch we tasted wines at a neighbouring wine shop but they seemed fiery and immature. We ordered a barrel of white and then continued on our way along the coast, intending to pick it up on our return. We motored for miles through the same delightful cliff scenery, only once meeting another party of Texas Rangers by the roadside. None of them seemed to know how far one could go before reaching the front line. Only an occasional Stars and Stripes topping a mountain pinnacle indicated that the war had passed this way. We even saw some Italians in sunglasses and bathing suits coming up from a beach.

As we neared the end of the Salerno peninsula, Dickie and I became more and more excited. Could it be that this steep coast road, so obviously easy to defend, had thus been overlooked by both sides? Was it possible to motor round the corner through Sorrento and into

Naples itself? There was not a sign of a soldier anywhere. However, just as we neared the end of the peninsula beyond Positano we suddenly came to a blown-up bridge, making further progress impossible. A GI standing beside the rubble informed us it had been destroyed to prevent a German counter-attack.

There was nothing left now but to return to Salerno with our barrel of wine and for me to join a supply convoy going back to the Battalion after nightfall. Like a schoolboy returning after half-term, I wished the respite could have been longer. The barrel of wine was used to supplement a drinks party hosted by Support Company in the home of the local Fascist leader. He had been killed by a British shell while sheltering in a ditch beside his house. The Swiss Consul had been invited as guest of the evening. The party was a roaring success until the *signora* returned in the middle to find a guardsman making love to one of her maids in her back garden, all her wine consumed by hilarious officers and Sammy Houldsworth masquerading in her *robe de balle*. Tears flowed in all directions. *Brute Inglese!*

Clearly a bit of discipline now needed to be reinstated after the huge casualties sustained at Battipaglia. Colonel Guy Taylor, who had commanded Support Company at Medenine, therefore ordered a full battalion parade in the football stadium at Salerno. We turned out as smartly as we could in separate companies, with all the officers (including the new replacements) out in front. Everyone could thus see his own unit and, above all, the whole battalion to which he belonged. Colonel Guy gave an excellent address which struck just the right note; but the Brigadier's led to mutterings behind me in the ranks of 'Give him his DSO!'

With the capture of Hill 270 by the Coldstream Guards on the road to Avellino, a way north had now been opened up. The armour now passed through into the plains beyond and the Germans made a fighting retreat to their next main line of defence along the Volturno river.

Although Right Flank were not so well placed as Support Company when we moved up to this new battle line, we were much better off than the other three rifle companies. Our positions were situated somewhat to the rear and were protected from shelling by a huge limestone ridge ending in a steep escarpment. What German shells came our way therefore landed harmlessly below. Life was not unpleasant as we squatted beside our slit trenches on the olive terraces and tried to think up new ways of cooking our bully beef and compo rations. The former could be marinaded in red wine and we had eggs and bottled fruit from abandoned Italian farmhouses. Each of our slit trenches moreover had a waterproof groundsheet over the top to keep off the occasional rainstorm. Living entirely among them, I soon got to know all the men of my reconstituted platoon. My new guardsman orderly with whom I shared my trench was a young Scots-Canadian volunteer. There were also two or three desert veterans who had come all the way through from Sollum and who regaled me with tales of their late company commander, Major Johnny Macrae, DSO, who had been killed at the first Battle of Alamein. He had apparently rescued the company, when surrounded, by rushing straight at the Italians firing a Bren gun from the hip. There were other legends of the desert fighting. For all their grumbling and battle-weariness when out of the line, Right Flank obviously still kept their fighting spirit and retained a high opinion of their invincibility if allowed to get within reach of the enemy.

For the first time our company positions here adjoined those of the Americans. At nightfall some of their GIs used to move into a cave just below us, where their presence served to remind us that we all now formed part of the American 5th Army under General Mark Clark. However, unless one was right alongside them, one was not aware of this. They obviously had an entirely separate sense of national identity quite apart from their military ones. They also seemed more nationalistic, displaying the Stars and Stripes everywhere – whereas we never flew the Union Jack.

The day drew near now for the crossing of the River Volturno, which was to be a concerted effort along the whole front of the 5th Army. The British 46th Division was to cross near the mouth of the river; an infantry brigade attached to the British 7th Armoured Division in the centre; and the Americans on our right. D-Day was to be 12 October 1943. Prior thereto we spent one sunny afternoon bathing and playing boats in the large lake at the back of Caserta Palace – a copy of Versailles once occupied by the Bourbon Kings of Naples and where Allied Headquarters were now ensconced. This was meant to be a practice for the crossing of the Volturno but I fully intended, if required, to swim my platoon the small distance across, as some of our patrols had already done, instead of staying bunched together like sitting ducks in canvas boats.

Colonel Guy held an order group the day before the crossing from which it transpired that only 'G' Company was to be involved in the initial assault. They were to make a mock attack across the river so as to draw the whole of the enemy's fire for an hour before the main crossing was made by the Americans further to the east. The entire corps artillery was to protect 'G' Company by firing a ten-minute barrage onto the further bank. The role of the Brigade was therefore diversionary; but we were thereafter to form the spearhead of the advance on the other side once a bridgehead had been secured.

There was some banter with the 'G' Company officers when we emerged from Colonel Guy's order group which, like all his conferences, he managed to make friendly and light-hearted. One of them said to me afterwards, 'You're just jealous because we're all going to win MCs tomorrow!'

Next day we could sit back in our grandstand positions on higher ground to watch the warlike overture before the curtain was raised on yet another phase of the Italian campaign.

It was a perfect day, so perfect that the artillery of both sides even seemed to have stopped firing as if it were wrong to disturb the autumnal peace. The leaves hung motionless on the trees. Zero hour was at 2000 hours. As the evening wore on I made my way with my platoon sergeant slowly up the mountain behind. It might have formed a background to a painting by Leonardo da Vinci as the sinking sun lit its rocky pinnacles with a contrasting brilliance. We continued along a goat track bordered by asphodels to watch the final setting of the sun into the western sea, lighting the domes of Capua while the Isle of Ischia floated in a pool of golden light.

Night was falling fast now and soon the brilliance faded, hiding first the valleys and then the mountain slopes in darkness. The bell in the ancient church of St Angelo was tolling the peasants to vespers through its graveyard bordered by cypress trees. Now it was pitch dark and the silence was disturbed only by the grating of the crickets. The second hand of my watch ticked gradually towards 8 p.m. I counted 'Five, four, three, two, one' – when suddenly the whole plain below erupted with stabbing flame. In an instant the peace of centuries was shattered by all the might of twentieth-century science. For brief instants church domes, roofs, village streets and treetops were here and there illumined by flashes from neighbouring gun pits. Closer at hand one could even catch momentary glimpses of gun crews servicing their field pieces in the bright light from their muzzles. The combined effect was as if the whole plain had been ignited.

We stared stupefied and as delighted as schoolboys at the sight of this inferno. The whole of the 5th Army's artillery was now in action; but most impressive of all, being nearest to us, was our own corps artillery firing a ten-minute barrage on to the further bank in support of 'G' Company. This involved three field guns in support of every guardsman and was said to be the biggest concentration of artillery fire since the Battle of Alamein.

Total casualties were ten sheep. Except for running into a minefield, our men encountered no difficulty whatsoever, saw no enemy and, after staying on the further bank for the scheduled hour, returned according to plan. The rest of us could have crossed through them without any difficulty.

But the main divisional crossing was still to be made, according to plan, by other bridges further down the river. The Germans, now realising what was up from the subsequent shifting of our artillery barrage, paid no more attention to 'G' Company but turned every field piece and Nebelwerfer (multi-barrelled mortar) they possessed on to that sector. For half an hour they strafed ours and their own bank and completely broke up the crossing, sinking ten boats. From our vantage point we could see the conflagration of bursting German shells and the Spandau tracer bouncing off the near bank. 46th Division eventually crossed after some bitter fighting and managed to maintain their positions despite fierce counter-attacks. On our right the Americans crossed without any difficulty and with nothing like the same weight of artillery support. The Volturno was much narrower on their front but they wisely chose not to encourage German reaction by warning barrages and more sensibly merely swam across with the aid of petrol-tin floats. Then, after knocking out two or three German Spandaus, they secured a bridgehead and had a pontoon bridge erected before the morning.

Next day 201 Guards Brigade crossed on this American bridge to secure the American's left flank and capture a chain of mountains to the north along which we now began to make our way. This involved a fifteen-mile trek carrying all our equipment and in the evening we dug in under spasmodic shellfire on the slopes of a mountain ridge. A black GI was sheltering near me in a slit trench and kept up a delightful banter as each salvo descended, shouting: 'Boss, here I go', as he ducked, to be followed immediately as he emerged again by, 'Boss, here I come.' He was one of the many blacks now serving in the American armed forces whose presence did more than anything else, since the abolition of slavery, to create an inclusive black and white

American consciousness. Nevertheless there were, as yet, no black American officers to be seen and the 'coloured troops' commanded by white officers were kept in separate contingents.

That night my platoon was sent on standing patrol to a ruined castle which dominated the hill above. It was difficult to approach without being seen, which we must have been as the Germans started mortaring the area from the other side. I moved my patrol slightly to one side of the track. This was as well because an hour later a machine-gun suddenly opened up and sprayed the whole track with bullets, trying to make us reveal our positions. I was afraid someone was going to get hit, for we were not entrenched. But our luck held and silence settled once more over the mountains. It was bitterly cold at this height, and the October moon seemed to hang stationary as we crouched with fingers on triggers peering ahead into the menacing darkness. At long last the moon set and the first pale light of dawn began to illumine the weary faces of my men and enable us to relax. Then as the sun rose we descended the hill to rejoin the rest of the company and eat a hearty breakfast in the expectation of being able to make up for lost sleep. But it was not to be. As so often, one had to prepare to move on regardless of fatigue.

Anthony Balfour, my new company commander, now wanted me at Company Headquarters to give orders for the advance. We had to march further up the valley and form up for an attack with the other two battalions of the Brigade who were already entrenched there. Apparently this chain of steep mountains stretching due north for about twenty miles was to be captured by advancing from crest to crest thus also forcing the Germans to withdraw from the surrounding plain.

Just before we set off, a member of another platoon managed to set himself alight from head to foot when pouring petrol on to his brew can fire. The poor fellow foolishly poured it straight out of a two-gallon can on to the flames which then ran up the stream of liquid and exploded the can in his face. We wrapped him up like an Egyptian mummy, silent, though still breathing, and placed him on a jeep for transportation to the rear. His platoon officer was completely shaken by this incident. A poet and short-story writer, this officer was one of those unmilitary (though often brave) individuals who somehow managed to obtain a wartime commission. He regarded the whole war business as sheer lunacy. Indeed one wondered why he had not been a conscientious objector. Having only just joined the

Battalion he now proceeded to behave in such a way that one did not know whether he was being deliberately funny, or was mad, or merely 'bomb happy'. He had brought with him a tin trunk containing not military equipment, but scores of books on poetry and philosophy to prevent him from getting bored. As he appeared on arrival to have no defensive weapons, I lent him a spare tommy-gun from my platoon, whereupon he had asked me in front of my men, 'Which of these damn knobs do I press to make the damn thing fire?'

For the ensuing attack, his platoon was to be in reserve and Paddy Bowen-Colthurst's and mine were to take the lead. We climbed up the final ridge to our start-line in a torrential downpour which while soaking us also screened our movements. The rain continued to shield us as we advanced in extended line with fixed bayonets across a boulder-strewn valley on to our objective. It was only when our two leading platoons were almost there that the rain clouds suddenly lifted and a brilliant sun emerged. The attack was then momentarily interrupted by some Italians trying to sell us apples! When they had been sent away and the reserve platoon was coming up from behind to join us, a German machine-gun which, owing to the rain, had not seen us before, suddenly opened up on them. The other platoon, who were now without cover, began running towards us in a way that might charitably be described as 'advancing' until they were able to take refuge behind some rocks and boulders. Their officer with his usual warped humour said he had been waving a white handkerchief at the Germans to stop them shooting, but unfortunately they hadn't seen him. My company commander, who overheard this remark, was not in the least amused and indeed this proved to be the end of our junior poet's command. I later learned that he then spent a few days in a base hospital, where he created such an uproar that he was certified mad and removed to North Africa.

The mountainside was now pure rock and proved impossible to excavate for slit trenches; so we followed the German example of constructing circular sangars of loose stones to give some protection against bullets and flying shrapnel. Two shells landed right in the middle of my platoon position. Although no Germans were to be seen, this was no place for relaxed precautions as the enemy were still in occupation of the village of Baronissi just below. They were dislodged by 'G' Company and Left Flank next morning after a stiff fight.

As we later learned, the Germans certainly had something here to defend and conceal, namely the burial place of a horde of civilians they had brutally massacred. The hostility which caused this terrible slaughter had apparently been aroused when a German soldier raped an Italian girl; and her lover, according to the law of retaliation, promptly shot the rapist. The German infantry company then occupying the village took this as an insult to themselves, demanding vengeance against the village population. As we later learnt from the subsequent war trial, all the menfolk of the village were then shepherded together, including their two Roman Catholic priests, and marched under military escort to a volcanic depression forming a natural quarry. Here they were made to stand while from ground level above the German troops fired volley after volley into the packed mass until all were dead or dying. Then to conceal the crime and to save the trouble of burial, the sides of the declivity were simply dynamited in on them. Here the Battalion now discovered their pitiable remains.

In the course of the afternoon, while my platoon remained entrenched above the village, a solitary man appeared on the skyline just as I was giving orders to my sections. He ran down the hill towards us stopping and sinking to his knees every few yards with his hands clasped in prayerful thanks, shouting 'Salvare! Salvare!' These exclamations he stopped and repeated every fifty yards as he descended the mountainside towards me while I was addressing my men. As he completed the last lap he burst through my surrounding cluster of men and seized me round the knees. He was one of the few survivors of the massacre.

At this point the company runner came up, saluted me and said, 'You're wanted at Company Headquarters for an order group right away, sir!' I felt the usual weak feeling in the pit of my stomach. What was it to be next, patrol or attack?

I joined the other two platoon commanders at Company Headquarters where we now received our orders. We were to move off at 11 p.m. Another battalion of the brigade had taken up the advance, had run into trouble and were now entrenched on a ridge some five miles ahead from where we were to attack strong enemy positions at dawn. Apparently we were now closing in on the first outposts of the new German 'Winter Line'.

We marched off into the moonlit darkness. All went well until the last mile when clouds obscured the moon and we got temporarily lost trudging through sodden ground where we sank in up to our gaiters.

It was 3 a.m. and felt like the Slough of Despond. Then we climbed up a stony track onto the ridge above where the other battalion were entrenched. It was about 4.50 a.m. as we lined up in front of them for the attack with 'G' Company on the left. H Hour was to be in ten minutes but half the company now fell asleep from utter exhaustion and we had to go round shaking them to their feet. Colonel Guy then asked the company commanders if they were ready and we stumbled off into the darkness which was just changing to dawn.

As we advanced it became apparent that, contrary to the contours shown on our very inaccurate Italian maps, the sides of this mountain were precipitous and the top of the ridge correspondingly narrower than originally supposed. Our two companies thus became entangled and had to advance in three waves practically shoulder to shoulder as if in the Crimean War. We were protected, however, by an accurate artillery barrage from our artillery covering the last few hundred yards.

Then a complete anti-climax – the Germans had just withdrawn. We took over their positions just as dawn was breaking and found not a soul in sight except for three deserters in a house below who emerged with hands above their heads when we burst open the door. I lay down in one of the German sangars, placed a cape over the roof as a shield against the rising sun, and fell instantly asleep.

I only remained so for half an hour. Then I was roughly shaken and ordered to report immediately to the Commanding Officer. In his usual friendly way Colonel Guy asked me to climb on to the next mountain crest to see if it was occupied by the enemy. It would, he explained, save a lot of trouble as, if unoccupied, he did not require to lay on a full battalion attack.

I chose only two men to accompany me and, as there was not a vestige of cover, arranged for another platoon to protect us with mortar smoke if seen to be fired upon. But we arrived on the next mountain crest without incident, apart from the sight of some Germans running down the reverse slope who must have been a standing patrol. The rest of the Battalion now followed in our wake over the next ridge and then down to the foothills below, where we again came under heavy artillery fire. An obvious advantage that the Germans had in this mountain terrain, so admirably suited to defence, was that whenever they retired to their next main line they had all our likely positions registered for artillery fire. At this stage of the Italian campaign they must indeed have caused us far more casualties

[67]

than we did them. So much for Churchill's 'soft underbelly of the Axis'. The Germans were also now opposing us with more divisions than we had.

Next day the enemy shelling became severe and it was obvious from their coordinated fire plan that we were now coming up against part of their Winter Line. Shells whistled incessantly overhead, interspersed with the whining of the Nebelwerfer mortars – which we called 'moaning minnies' from the noise they made. Left Flank on a higher ridge behind came in for the worst of this and suffered sixteen casualties in a very short time. One of their platoon positions seemed continuously enveloped by bursting shells and I could see their stretcher-bearers running about to remove their casualties.

Situated in front and behind a steep ridge, Right Flank were better protected; but as none of our (unarmed) Basuto porters would carry supplies through this heavy bombardment we were now without food, water or blankets.

While my company commander was away at an order group an urgent request now came through from Left Flank for the loan of our stretchers – there being only two to each company. I was loathe to release more than one as the regimental aid post was situated three miles back down a mountain track. Almost immediately after one stretcher had gone a salvo landed right on top of us, badly wounding one of the signallers and a company runner. The signaller's leg was smashed beyond repair, so I injected him with morphia and sent him back; but we could only tie up the other poor fellow's wounds and leave him lying crying intermittently for help. He was silent and deathly white when the stretcher was eventually returned some two hours later.

The most distressing feature of suffering casualties under these conditions was the difficulty of evacuating the wounded, many of whom needlessly died. Half a dozen casualties in a platoon could occupy the remainder with their evacuation. It also has a demoralising effect on front-line troops to spend so long with their wounded and dying.

201 Guards Brigade, whose reputation had been made as motorised infantry during the desert campaign, were now having to make all the improvisations they could for warfare on mountain tops. We even formed a mule team of our own consisting of commandeered Italian mules to take heavy supplies up the mountains. Any guardsman with farming experience was roped in as a muleteer. This worked

comparatively well considering that none of them had ever tried to control a mule before. We also had some Italian volunteer carriers as well as the black Basutos from South Africa already mentioned. The latter, who were all volunteers, now managed to get through to us on our ridge after dark, each carrying a blanket slung over his shoulder with a water can tied to each end and a food box on his head. They were not, however, allowed to carry weapons and were only guarded by a single British sergeant armed with a revolver. They were a most welcome sight.

Next day it at last started to rain turning the tracks to mud; but later in the evening we received the welcome news that the whole battalion was about to be pulled out of the line for a rest. We certainly needed it. One only had to look around the company to see their bloodshot eyes with black rings of exhaustion and three days' growth of beard – for there was, of course, no water for shaving.

Our positions were now taken over by a brand new brigade from North Africa still wearing the khaki drill uniforms in which they had been rushed over as reinforcements. We marched down the mountain to a village about two miles to the rear where we obtained blankets and lay down in long lines round a field to make up for lost sleep.

Next day the order was for a shave and general clean-up, to be followed by platoon inspections. It was after lunch, however, that we received the bombshell news and sudden reversal of orders. There was to be no respite after all. The Corps Commander had asked for one final effort to break through the German line by capturing Monte Santa Croce, just in front and which was reckoned to be the main strongpoint of the intermediate German Line. The enemy had now to be kept on the run, to prevent him consolidating.

The Grenadier battalion were to take Monte Croce itself, protected by covering fire from my battalion, who were then to attack and take the defended hilltop town of Rocchetta just below. Owing to the difficulties of getting up ammunition and other supplies and the unpredictability of our porters under fire, the unusual course was adopted of using the Coldstream battalion as temporary porters for the other two battalions.

The Grenadiers had been working their way along the foothills towards Monte Croce for the last day or two and were now near their start-line. We, however, who had been advancing further to the west, were down again at the bottom of the valley and would have to spend the night climbing back up the 1,000-foot escarpment to be ready for the next day's attack. After hearing this news I went and sat down by myself in an olive grove. We had been messed around enough and I simply could not bring myself at first to tell my platoon. It seemed incomprehensible. They had been promised a rest and were now at last drying out sodden clothes and attending to raw and blistered feet. Soldiers cannot climb and fight for days with no opportunity to wash or change socks or clothing without taking the physical consequences. There were now queues of guardsmen outside the regimental aid post to have their shrapnel wounds dressed. Despite the Medical Officer's objections Colonel Guy now shut the RAP except for the seriously wounded. In the circumstances we required discipline, not sympathy.

Later I gave out my orders to a hushed and weary platoon. They took the news remarkably well, knowing there was nothing else to be done but to comply with orders and try to maintain the name of the Battalion and the Regiment. *Esprit de corps* was all we had to hold us together.

When the moon rose the Battalion climbed silently to and fro up a sheep track (marked by white tape) which zig-zagged up the steep escarpment as we stumbled and climbed from the dark valley towards the starlit plateau 1,000 feet above. At one moment someone carrying a mortar threw it down cursing from sheer desperation – then thought better of it and continued on his upward course. Hours later we gained the summit with only the sound of officers and NCOs congratulating the heavier laden and the unfit who had managed to reach the top. The moon was sinking now as we lay down in long lines among the hazel coppices to wait for dawn to break. Wisps of mountain mist covered the ranks of sleeping guardsmen, enfolding our bodies as in funeral shrouds. Not a word broke the silence, for we were absolutely dead beat.

When the sun rose we wound our way in long columns through the hazel and gorse bushes, dew-spangled and gossamered, along tracks pink with cyclamen, to where the Germans were supposed to be. Perhaps the enemy might have withdrawn again.

In a clearing we encountered Brigadier Gascoigne, a Grenadier, who spoke to me as we passed. He reassuringly told me the men of his regiment were already on Monte Croce to our right which they had occupied without difficulty. The peak rose in alpine glory above our heads and must have involved them in a goat-like climb but apparently with no opposition. Its very remoteness, however, indicated that it would be quite impossible for them to give us any covering fire as we now advanced on Rocchetta. Our inadequate Italian maps of this region gave no indication that the Grenadiers would be separated from us by over 1,000 vertical feet.

The little town of Rocchetta was now visible considerably below us, involving a downhill approach along a track which cut into the side of the mountain and was lined with impenetrable scrub, giving little opportunity to deploy on either side. Down this narrow line of advance, Left Flank and 'G' Companies now advanced in broad daylight with the latter company leading. The Germans entrenched on the ridge above Rocchetta let them proceed unimpeded for some distance until they had them bunched together and then they suddenly opened fire. The leading platoon commander and most of his front section were instantly killed. At first I heard a few bursts of Spandau, then a whole crescendo of firing as a dozen machine-guns opened up on them. There was fearful carnage. Our men were in desperate plight as those who were not casualties could neither advance nor retire with the Germans firing at anyone who raised his head. The Grenadiers were not, of course, in a position to give them any covering fire. None of the score of wounded could be extricated and were left lying beside the dead. Some stretcher-bearers managed to reach Sammy Houldsworth, the company commander of Left Flank, and inject him with morphia; but when placed on a stretcher he was promptly shot again.

The Brigadier, to whom I had just spoken (as usual right up at the front), now ordered Colonel Guy to press forward immediately with my company along the same – and only – narrow line of advance. This Colonel Guy declined to do. The Brigadier then said that if that was the case he would have to order his own regiment (the Grenadiers on our right) to do so. But their commanding officer, Colonel Billy Kingsmill, apparently replied that if our battalion could not do so, nor would he. I was up beside them at this awkward juncture and heard some remarks about Colonel Guy being sent away on some course which he referred to as 'quite a Cook's tour'.

Later as it grew dark, I found Colonel Guy, who now appeared to have completely 'lost his name' with our irascible Brigadier, sitting disconsolately on a rocky outcrop above Rocchetta planning the Battalion's night attack on the German defences below. This was how the attack should have been mounted originally. My company was to overrun the German positions under cover of darkness and take the hill dominating Rocchetta in the middle of the valley. 'F' Company were then to clear Rochetta itself and 'G' Company – or what was left of it – was to follow through and take the mountain ridge beyond. The men were falling asleep now in the assembly area so my new company commander, Anthony Balfour, allowed benzedrine to be issued to keep them awake.

It was pitch dark when we started to advance downhill as the artillery put down a smokescreen to conceal us. My platoon was in reserve this time. There was some wild and inaccurate mortar fire from the Germans as we groped our way through the remnants of 'G' Company. It was obvious that they were completely out of action for their casualties littered the ground and all their able-bodied were now helping to extricate the wounded on improvised stretchers of great-coats and rifles. It would be a long haul back for their wounded and I was glad the darkness hid their sufferings.

Once past 'G' Company, several enemy machine-guns opened fire on us from below with tracer bullets. A sergeant shouted, 'Keep going, lads, keep going!' as the eighty-odd men of Right Flank groped their way downwards with words of mutual encouragement. A man here or there faltered and ducked. It was certainly unpleasant advancing downhill like this in the dark towards the source of these glowing tracer bullets, which as they rose towards us weaved intricate patterns and seemed to converge at the very pit of one's stomach – although they mostly passed thirty feet overhead. We appeared to be descending into the very jaws of death. But the guardsmen maintained excellent formation with the repeated refrain of 'Keep going, lads, keep going!' We were conscious that we had to maintain the name of the Battalion.

We eventually reached the flat ground below the escarpment on the top of which the Germans were entrenched. Perhaps they thought we were retiring and merely using the darkness and smokescreen to evacuate our dead and wounded. More likely, however, we were now in dead ground beneath their line of fire. For whatever reason they stopped shooting just as we reached the fields below them and deployed at last for the final assault.

We could now see above us the dim shape of the hill, which was our objective. It was pitch dark down below and quiet, for the moon had not yet risen and the Spandaus had stopped firing. We lay down in long ranks among the shell craters waiting for the final command to attack. I thought I could hear muttered German voices on either side and even fancied I could smell their cigars – so acutely were one's senses attuned to the surroundings. I almost longed for something to happen to break the suspense. Still, strangely, nothing did.

Suddenly Tony Balfour gave a quiet word of command and we rose up in line and moved across the open to our objective without a shot being fired. But the enemy had seen us at last. I had just got my platoon into their final position on the reverse slope of the hill, and Tony had just begun to ascend with 8 Platoon round the left, when several Spandaus opened fire all at once. Simultaneously there were a series of shots overhead, and a shower of red sparks from an exploding hand grenade. Lit up by its flash Tony appeared outlined for a brief instant above, shouting to me, 'Come up quickly, for God's sake!'

The whole company then went quite berserk. We started charging round the flank of the hill swearing like madmen and almost artificially furious with the enemy above who made us feel so frightened. Then our courage soared as we closed in on the summit, clambering over rocks, getting stuck on ledges and then extricating ourselves. 9 Platoon was now all mixed up with my own, yelling, 'Come on, Right Flank!' and finally, 'Come on the Battalion!' as surmounting the crest we leaped on those terrified Germans who stood their ground. There was no withstanding the company once its blood was up. Our shouts of 'Come on out and fight, you bastards!' to the surrounding trenches and dug-outs could be even heard by battalion headquarters up the hill; but any Germans who did so were promptly bayoneted. I never saw Right Flank in so ferocious a mood. It was as if all the pent-up fury at the shelling, the casualties and not being able to get one's own back was at last to have its vengeance. When the bloody combat was over I went out to try and get a machine-gun post in front which had been firing at us. Paddy Bowen-Colthurst went for another. But both crews had now fled, abandoning their guns in terror. The Germans also left a completely laden mule train in front and abandoned the town of Rocchetta on our left, which 'F' Company entered later in the night without opposition. We could hear shouts and clattering of equipment on the next ridge from which another German company appeared to be withdrawing.

Right Flank were now fighting mad and all for doing another bayonet attack. But this was 'G' Company's objective. At this moment we felt we could have taken on the whole German army!

However, we had new sangars to construct of boulders (one could not dig trenches here) and also our casualties to attend to. A full moon rose over the landscape and bathed all the mountains in its clear metallic light. Beside my sangar was revealed the corpse of a guardsman from the leading section of 8 platoon with a neat row of bullet holes across his chest. He must have been shot by Schmeisser automatic at very close range. Ronnie, his platoon officer, was lying groaning in another pit where we had placed him for protection. He had a nasty stomach wound. As our stretchers had been commandeered on the way by 'G' Company, there was no means of evacuating him for several hours. I had to give him two morphia injections before the stretcher-bearers returned from their four-mile trek. Tony told me he had been lucky: when grenades had been thrown at him on the summit, he had fired five shots at one German with his revolver and missed each time.

When the stretcher-bearers had evacuated all our wounded and finally returned for the German casualties, one of the latter had died from his bayonet wounds. The bayonet is a cruel weapon as every man bayoneted is a potential prisoner. But our men were still trained to use cold steel and a bayonet charge certainly strikes fear into the enemy.

Eventually we settled down to try to get such sleep as all this excitement would allow. I never saw the full moon shine so brilliantly. Its unflinching light transformed these grey jagged peaks into a bare and lunar landscape. Between fits of slumber I watched the moon go down.

Then, at last, came a soldier's dawn. The sun rose in blazing splendour to illumine all the Apennines. It was a glorious autumn day but, at this early hour, the plains below remained in a sea of cloud. Looking down on them from our heights, with the warmth of early sunlight on our faces, we felt like gods.

During the course of next morning I received a message to report at once to Company Headquarters. I was required to occupy the ridge in front, which we had been prevented from attacking the night before, but from which the Germans nevertheless appeared to have withdrawn. I advanced cautiously towards it with my platoon, covered by the guns of the other two platoons from the hill behind. Everywhere lay abandoned enemy weapon pits. In the deep valley dividing the two hills we also found some abandoned pack mules tethered to olive trees or grazing peacefully amidst the welter of abandoned equipment. It looked like a splendid looting party. On our objective were more platoon positions apparently abandoned like the rest with rucksacks lying all around. The enemy certainly seemed to have departed in a hurry.

Having halted my platoon just below the final ridge, I walked forward with my section commanders to site their new positions. In so doing I came over the brow where there were more rows of stone sangars apparently deserted like the rest. Suddenly a white face topped by a ginger mop of hair appeared over a parapet only thirty yards ahead. We gaped at each other for a brief instant. Without a helmet the individual did not look a bit like a German. Then I quickly fired my tommy-gun from the hip shouting 'Hands up!' in German; but my weapon jammed. Cursing I recocked it and fired one round, when it jammed again. Then there was a deafening crackle of German machine-gun bullets all round my ears. How they missed me at such close range I do not know. I leapt backwards into dead ground and retreated to join my platoon while the rest of the company on the hill behind fired at German heads popping up along the line of the ridge. With a large audience now watching from all sides, I laid on a model battle drill attack 'according to the book' with one covering section, two flanking sections and 2-inch mortar smoke. Our battle-school attack, however, was somewhat assisted by the complete withdrawal of the enemy who had by now retreated down the reverse slope. Last night had obviously been too much for them.

Our new positions on this new mountain top gave us a stupendous view northwards into the plains beyond. Indeed we seemed to have driven a salient into the middle of the German Winter Line. To the north-west and 1,000 feet below our ridge I could see a number of Germans. The nearest were occupying positions about 1,000 yards away and impossible to shoot at with accuracy; our position above them, however, must have made them feel extremely uncomfortable. From our mountain position I could even now see behind the German lines into the plains beyond stretching for many miles to Monte Camino and Cassino – the obvious next line for defence. Through my binoculars I could even see part of the German artillery lines; including a battery of 88 mms. The exact position of each gun was revealed by a puff of smoke each time it fired. They must have been about three miles away. By wireless and through Battalion HQ I tried to get our corps artillery to range on them; but could not spot a single visible ranging shell from which to give adequate directions.

However, they must have been disturbed, as shortly afterwards they limbered up and withdrew.

It seemed that the Germans really were pulling out now that we had gained such a dominating feature. This was obvious too next morning when through my binoculars I could see no sign of any Germans in their former positions, from which they had clearly now withdrawn. I reported this back through Company Headquarters. Nevertheless a full-scale attack by a new brigade from North Africa, supported by all the divisional artillery, had already been laid on to clear the ridge below us to the west. There was, however, no one on it. We decided to deepen our trenches to protect ourselves before our needless barrage came down. It was as well we did so, for when our artillery opened up shells started landing all over the place and the sky was full of airbursts. I prayed that none would hit my platoon as the whole of the ridge to our left went up in fountains of smoke. Lines of infantry from the other brigade now appeared below us advancing behind the barrage. Suddenly some of the guns ranged on to another platoon of Right Flank whom they may have mistaken for Germans as they were wearing captured enemy greatcoats to keep warm. Before the guns could be stopped firing two of our men had been killed and two wounded.

When the other brigade had successfully passed through and down the further slope we became officially disengaged from the enemy and could scout around for something to eat. Here indeed was loot galore: cigars and *vino*, tins of coffee, not to mention German greatcoats and blankets which we badly needed, having far outrun our own supplies and even the gallant Basuto carriers. We found a mailbag containing parcels of woollen comforts and confectionery, including a child's christening cake. Before sending the mailbag back to our intelligence officer I tried to translate some of the letters it contained. The sentiments were just like those of our own men whose letters from the front line it was an officer's unpleasant duty to censor.

Being short of any meat to eat, we shot a sheep with one of our rifles which we then butchered and roasted on an open fire. It was as tough as old leather.

The best piece of looting, however, was done by 'F' Company at the expense of Divisional Headquarters who tried to send an Italian spy through their lines loaded with thousands of lira for the Italian Communist partisans. Thinking they were the more deserving recipients, or not perhaps believing the wretched fellow's story, they divested him of every penny he possessed.

When we had gathered all our loot together, it was time to descend the mountain again to the Battalion's rest area. Our heavy equipment and other loot was heaped on to the backs of the captured German mules. Then in a long line, filthy and bearded like pards, many wearing enemy greatcoats and equipment or carrying newly captured German Schmeisser automatics, we made our way downhill – feeling uncommonly pleased with ourselves.

5

Hospital Interlude

Colonel Guy Taylor was now leaving the Battalion after his recent row with the Brigadier, ostensibly for a staff course which had been arranged for him in England. To a man we were sorry to see him go. Always natural and cheerful, he inspired us with confidence. He had an inborn ability to identify himself with those he led and we correspondingly respected him as our leader. Indeed it was this over-identification that had just led him to lose his name by flatly refusing to mount an immediate second daylight attack on Rocchetta. For he was never concerned with making his name at our expense. I could imagine that this might not always recommend him to some superiors. With him too went the last of the desert commanders. Brigadier Julian in contrast was known (perhaps unjustly) as 'Butcher Gascoigne' by the guardsmen for having caused his Grenadier battalion at Mareth in North Africa to continue attacking the German line over an extensive minefield which had not been cleared beforehand. As a result they had lost nearly all their platoon officers as well as scores of guardsmen.

The casualties so far incurred by the Battalion had now been heavy and must have seemed doubly so to these veterans who had been through it all before in North Africa. Between landing at Salerno on 9 September 1943 and the present date at the end of October we had already lost 304 other ranks and 27 officers killed, wounded or missing. The lightly wounded, however, tended to return once they had recovered in hospital.

It was now to hospital that, although unwounded, I was ordered to go by my company commander, with the connivance of Colonel Guy. I was suffering like so many others from a worsening dysentery which had not improved over the last few days – despite all the exhilaration. The Battalion was anyway due for a rest along with the rest of 201 Guards Brigade and was expected to be out of the line for some time.

It was with mixed feelings therefore that I found myself in a casualty clearing station in a bombed school some miles behind the front. A starvation diet of hot tea and morphia pills was expected to cure my inglorious complaint, while I lay on a stretcher amidst the genuine wounded and the stench of putrefying flesh. One man died in the room. In the next bed I found as company a man from Left Flank who was in considerable pain from a horrible wound he had received when lying on a stretcher. Sometimes when he cried for help I had to minister to his needs, for the male orderlies were an idle lot who seemed to have grown impervious to all the suffering around them. In contrast the doctors and surgeons worked like Trojans trying to keep up with the flow of casualties.

The hospital was situated in a converted Italian barracks near Capua which bore an enormous Fascist inscription around its central compound: 'War is to Man what maternity is to Woman'. In a separate room beside my ward was a young German officer shot severely in both legs. Our Medical Corps were now nursing him back to health after we had failed to kill him. He told me he had been wounded and taken prisoner by the Americans when patrolling across the Rapido river. Before that he had been temporarily captured by the Canadians in Sicily but had then escaped. He now proudly displayed his Iron Cross in a leather case beside his bed. The British nurses did not seem to like him and said he was a proper young Nazi. But the hospital padre had befriended him and had given him a book to read entitled *Deutschen Feldherren*!

After a few days I could stand the putrid atmosphere no longer and, feeling somewhat out of place among all these genuine wounded, I persuaded the harassed medical officer to give me a box of his dysentery pills and allow me to stay with the Battalion's 'B' Echelon which happened to be nearby with Battalion transport and all the supernumerary officers. This, however, made things worse again as food and wine flowed, so I soon found myself back this time in a general hospital for dysentery patients at Naples. Here were many others suffering from acute enteritis or jaundice; and one could receive proper medication and be looked after by nursing sisters. It had been pouring incessantly for the whole of the past week and as I lay in the security of my bed listening to the rain thundering on the hospital roof or hissing in the Naples gutters, I felt thankful I was not crouching in a sodden slit trench or floundering up mountain tracks that must by now be raging torrents.

Word now came through that the Battalion had been done out of their promised rest as the 56th (London) Division had moved up to the next German defence line to keep the enemy on the run. Their objective this time was the 3,000-foot massif of Monte Camino with its two subsidiary peaks, just beside Cassino. It was hoped the Germans might yield without serious fighting, thereby permitting the Allies to straighten their line right across Italy and bring them up to the much-vaunted German Gustav Line – yet another part of the so-called 'soft underbelly of the Axis'. The enemy, however, had no intention of yielding Monte Camino without a bitter struggle. Its great monastery hill dominated Route 7 and protected Cassino with its historic monastery behind. Here was the entrance to the Liri Valley – the traditional gateway to Rome.

The likely strength of the German defences round Monte Camino had by now already been observed and reported to Brigade Headquarters by one of my platoon. This was Guardsman Chadwick, prominent in the tobacco factory attack, who had also been taken prisoner along with me. Finding himself on a prison train south of Rome, he managed to jump off it when it was travelling round a bend so the German guards could not shoot. He then made his way southwards dressed as an Italian civilian, living with local people, until he came to the Camino region. Here he lived for about a week observing the German defensive preparations, including the blasting of rock shelters, until he finally arrived in the lines of the London Scottish where their Colonel was much surprised to be saluted 'as improperly dressed' by an apparent Italian. The Colonel took Chadwick to see the Brigadier who was much pleased with his detailed information and he was later awarded the DCM. When I met him at 'B' Echelon he had also just been granted three weeks' leave at the Brigadier's request. But his information about the prepared defences on Monte Camino were not apparently treated as sufficient warning of what to expect.

When the news of the new offensive came through on our hospital wireless I felt guilty lying in bed. All day long the wind howled and the rain pelted down, grounding our air force and turning the supply routes into seas of mud. Next afternoon news began to filter back of how the attack had been pressed up the 'razorback' ridge and its subsidiary peaks. All supplies had to be manhandled by Basutos or conveyed by mules as they had been during our attack on Rocchetta. Monastery Hill – so called from the battered monastery which the Germans held tenaciously – was also captured. But along the topmost ridges the Hermann Goering Division launched a series of savage counter-attacks. The brunt of these attacks fell on the Grenadiers and our 'F' company sent in to reinforce them.

It was two days later that the wounded began coming into our base hospital, having first passed through the local casualty clearing stations. Unless permanently incapacitated, the wounded went no further than Naples. At first they were mainly Grenadiers saying the whole of their battalion had been wiped out. This fortunately proved to be an exaggeration although they had suffered very severely and lost most of their platoon officers.

In the next hospital bed to me was a middle-aged Grenadier major, too old to be sitting in a flooded slit trench. He was suffering from acute arthritis which had so crippled him that he could hardly get out of his hospital bed. He was nevertheless fretting that he was not still up Monte Camino with his men; and, still more so, that he could not get out of bed to talk to the survivors now being carried by the score into the other ranks' wards. So as I was now beginning to recover and be allowed out of bed, I spent afternoons as his liaison officer, ascertaining all possible information from his men and seeing that they were supplied with all available comforts. A truck driver from his battalion who had to make routine visits to Naples was also charged to report to him personally. Whenever this character arrived in the ward he did so stamping his feet to attention and saluting smartly – to the evident amusement of all other occupants of the ward.

The many other Grenadier wounded I spoke to reported on a grim battle now taking place on Monte Camino. It was impressive too to see the effect upon these men of belonging to a famous regiment. They had withstood repeated German counter-attacks and, although greatly outnumbered, had still managed to hold on like grim death to the mountain top. At one time the enemy had overrun half their positions. The hardest-pressed of their companies was at one time commanded from a stretcher by a major who had both legs shattered by shellfire but refused to be evacuated.

I worried too for the name of my battalion and how they too had faced up to this repeated battering, knowing the morale of some of the overfought desert veterans. There were indeed quite a number of deserters in Naples at this time. Towards the end of the week some Scots Guardsmen were carried into the hospital and I was relieved to find their morale no worse than that of any others; which is to say, while they all showed traces of their ordeal, their morale and loyalty to the Regiment was still intact. By talking with the wounded I also learned that 'F' Company, now commanded by Richard Coke, after his Company Commander had been killed, had been moved up to reinforce the Grenadiers at a moment of crisis. An attack by a battalion of the Hermann Goering Division brought them swarming round 'F' Company's positions hurling grenades and calling upon them in vain to surrender. All the officers of 'F' Company became casualties with the exception of Richard Coke himself who deservedly won a DSO. Of the company's 105 men who climbed up the mountain, only 57 returned.

I now learned that a few guardsmen from Right Flank had been brought in as casualties. I walked round the wards in the hope of speaking to someone from my platoon. Whilst so doing I was shocked to be hailed by my Scots-Canadian guardsman orderly lying in bed with the bedclothes surmounting a cage where his leg should have been. I did not know what to say in sympathy, and felt most inadequate. He kept on flinching with pain and said he felt as if his foot was crushed – only it wasn't there. I learnt from him that the Company had suffered some casualties – from shelling. They had started the advance up the mountain with a successful charge in their best style, taking several prisoners. But when the main battle was engaged near the summit, they came under heavy shell fire which decimated my platoon in particular. It lost three officers in a row and my platoon sergeant had his leg shattered. Now it looked as if, when I returned, I would find a very different platoon.

I also learnt from other officers in the ward that the Brigadier had at last been awarded the DSO, which he doubtless deserved. He had now been severely wounded while, as usual, up with his forward groups in a fury with all these Germans holding up his Guards brigade. At the end of the week we heard that the whole of the 56th Division had been withdrawn off Monte Camino as well as the Americans off the adjacent Monte Luigo. The 5th Army commander had found it impossible to push on in the weakened condition to which the infantry divisions had now been reduced.

It was in the lull which occurred after the costly failure of the first Camino offensive that I was transferred to an officers' convalescent home at Sorrento, just south of Naples. From here one could hitch-hike into the city or take a boat across to the Isle of Capri – for the Americans had not yet commandeered it for their troops and put it out of bounds. There was not much left to see in Naples, so soon after its occupation, except for the black market and the brothels which had doubtless only closed for a night after the Germans left before reopening for their new clientele. The Americans, always the greater realists in such matters, had stuck up warning notices around the city stating: 'If she's game, she's got it. If she's got it, you've had it!'

I spent one night on Capri with Paddy Bowen-Colthurst from Right Flank, who was recuperating in hospital from a mixture of jaundice and malaria. We had the entire Hotel Paradiso in Anacapri to ourselves, with all its waiters in attendance. There was not a military soul in sight except for an Italian Alpini regiment now disarmed. We took two of their Alpini hats complete with goose feathers. In a neighbouring restaurant the proprietor produced a large bottle of Benedictine for us after an excellent dinner of fried squid and other Mediterranean delicacies. As the evening wore on the restaurant became empty until finally there were only two other civilians besides ourselves. When the proprietor had drinks with us we asked him to invite the two over to join us. He thereupon became embarrassed, saying that surely we would not wish to drink with German civilians. But Paddy and I were well away by this time and invited them to join our table.

One of the Germans turned out to be a Dr Otto Sohn-Rethel who was a portrait painter. He said his father had once painted a portrait of Queen Victoria and he talked with nostalgia of the old days and, trying to please us, of the contrasting barbarity of modern Nazi youth. I interrupted in my broken German to tell him teasingly that some people in Scotland regarded Prince Henry of Bavaria as Stuart successor to the British Throne. He became wildly excited as I explained the Jacobite custom of drinking to 'the King over the water' by passing the toasting glass, before drinking, over a finger bowl. The proprietor, who had initially attempted to disown his two old friends, now became enthusiastic and brought not only benedictine but also finger bowls filled with water for our disloyal toast. We then stood on the chairs with one foot on the table in Highland fashion; but my explanation in German had not been good enough, for our guests proceeded to drink all the water out of their finger bowls!

Back in Sorrento next day we called at Paddy's suggestion on the famous liberal philosopher Benedetto Croce, after having first telephoned him. As an anti-Fascist he was delighted to entertain two

British officers and gave us tea with his wife and charming daughters. The war seemed far away as we conversed with this most civilised and genuine of Italians.

6

Along the Garigliano

It was clearly time I returned to the Battalion. This meant first returning to 'B' Echelon, still situated near Rocchetta not far from where I had originally retired from the fray. Just arrived there from England to replace Colonel Guy was a new commanding officer who had formerly commanded the now disbanded 4th Battalion of the Regiment, with a posse of his own officers. Regimental headquarters had been forced to disband his battalion for use as reinforcements among the now decimated 1st and 2nd Battalions of the Regiment. Just before sailing for Salerno, 2SG had already received a small sprinkling of such reinforcements. Some, like myself, had at first resented their separate outlook and way of life; but the survivors, after three hard months of fighting, had by now become largely integrated. Each man's new company was now The Company to him, just as our battalion had now become The Battalion.

One of the disbanded 4th Battalion's companies sent out as reinforcements was kept intact and so joined us as a complete company. This new 'F' Company, unlike individual reinforcements, retained their own company identity but regretted leaving the disbanded 4th Battalion.

Another 4th Battalion company to remain intact without its individuals being dispersed around other battalions was 'S' Company, attached, as such, to a battalion of the Coldstream Guards who were also in need of reinforcements. As an independent company of the Regiment within a battalion of a different Guards regiment, they were placed on their mettle and conscious of the need to uphold the name of their regimental company among strangers. In these circumstances their loyalties were magnified at company rather than at battalion level with a fine *esprit de corps* of their own.

The group of 4th Battalion officers I now encountered on arrival at 'B' Echelon posed further loyalty problems. For they included not only the 4th Battalion's Commanding Officer as our new CO, but also their Adjutant and most of their former headquarters' staff.

Obviously peeved at losing their old battalion's name and number and unimpressed by their new surroundings, they talked as if my battalion needed to be reshaped into a pale reflection of their own. Doubtless there was much of which to be critical in our easy disregard for certain military conventions. I had felt just the same on first joining the Battalion at Tripoli. But I was now firmly identified with 2SG and its long fighting record running back to desert days with its different way of life and even of uniform. These Inglese newcomers – or 'Brown Jobs' as they were sometimes called – wore brown instead of black berets, and carried map cases, whistles, and notebooks so useful on home manoeuvres.

Part of the Battalion was now engaged in the second battle for Monte Camino. This had opened on 2 December 1943 with the heaviest concentration of artillery yet fired in the Italian campaign, with aerial bombardment and even with our ack-ack guns firing from ground level straight at the mountain top. The assault this time involved two army corps instead of one division and with the Americans attacking to the east. Before this overwhelming force the Germans now made a fighting withdrawal into the Gustav Line, abandoning Monte Camino, and so leaving British X Corps (as part of the American 5th Army) facing them along the line of the Garigliano river.

Rumours were now growing that the Battalion would shortly be sent home on 'the ship with the tartan funnel'; but for the moment 201 Guards Brigade was to be removed from 56 (London) Division and temporarily attached to a new British one just arrived in X Corps, for future operations along the Garigliano.

A week's rest and the Battalion therefore found itself in the line again, beside the flooded mouth of the Garigliano where I now rejoined them. Our positions down on the plain were not too bad and were infinitely preferable to the mountain tops now powdered with snow. Company and Battalion Headquarters were able to be situated inside farm houses and platoon slit trenches could be dug deep in the soft earth of the plain – so unlike the mountain rock on which we used to build our stone sangars.

No man's land in front was a sheet of flood water through which the River Garigliano flowed and which on our side was intersected by banked up roads. This area was inhabited by myriads of wild duck and geese which came flighting in at sunset over 'G' Company's positions amidst the sand dunes, the duck mainly in twos and threes and the greylag geese in thousands. We were forbidden to shoot at them for fear of revealing our positions. I could occasionally hear some German sportsmen, however, shooting with shotguns on the other side. One afternoon Corporal 'Swill' Bryson, MM, picked off four mallard with his captured Italian Beretta. There was a flooded patch of field just in front of my platoon positions simply black with duck. Seeking to emulate Corporal Bryson's performance I concealed two Bren guns about a hundred yards away and then fired a preliminary burst to make the duck rise which they did with a thunderclap of a thousand wings. For several seconds we poured volley after volley into the flying mass of duck but were crestfallen when only two birds came down. Clearly we needed proper shotguns.

The platoon of which I now assumed command was somewhat different from my previous one but was still in my old company, Right Flank. I never seemed to stay long enough with any platoon in Italy to be firmly conscious of being the commander of nos 7, 8 or 9 platoons. Also, owing to the high casualty rates, NCO promotion was apt to be from one platoon to another; and a degree of inter-changeability between the men of each platoon thus resulted. When an officer, like myself, came back from hospital, he usually returned to his old company to which he felt he belonged: but, rather than displace a new officer already installed, he would sometimes be shifted to command another platoon.

I was therefore more conscious of belonging to Right Flank than to any particular platoon. The platoon of which I was now, however, given command also contained some prize Battalion characters. My platoon sergeant, Sergeant Wilson, also known as 'Joe Plush', was a likeable rogue and a natural actor. He was a regular soldier like Corporal Bryson. All these old regulars seemed to have nicknames. Corporal 'Swill' Bryson had earned his MM in the 1st Battalion for shooting down a German plane in Norway at the very beginning of the war. He simply did not know the meaning of fear and regarded warfare (as he told me) as the greatest game on earth. He kept the whole of Right Flank roaring with laughter at his tales. Unfortunately he had been transferred to Company Headquarters when I arrived, ostensibly as company sniper, but he still used to return to my platoon for what he called his 'morale brew' of tea. When in the 1st Battalion of the Regiment he had apparently fallen out with his company commander, and was then transferred to the 2nd Battalion which he now regarded as his preferable home. We used to get a lot of misfits in this way, sent out by Regimental Head-quarters from home battalions, including some officers.

My new platoon had previously been commanded by Sir Iain Moncreiffe, a future Scottish Herald, who had now gone off sick. He used to twirl his moustaches saying 'Splendid!' to the men or 'Splendid, Sergeant Wilson, splendid!' whenever he found things to his satisfaction. He had been with them at the second Battle of Monte Camino. Now it had become a craze with my men and I would hear Joe Plush going the rounds saying 'Everything alright here?' – 'O.K., Sergeant'; then in reply 'Splendid, men, splendid!' with a twirl of his imaginary moustaches.

Iain was a considerable character with an encyclopaedic knowledge of the pedigrees of all the aristocratic families of Europe on both sides of the firing line. He had commanded the draft of Scots Guards reinforcements that I had accompanied on a cramped troopship all the way round the Cape of Good Hope. On disembarkation at Port Said the fighting in the desert had not quite ended. We were rightly judged to be quite unfit to be sent up to the front due to lack of exercise as well as excessive drinking while aboard. So all the officers were ordered to parade for a 'toughening up' course at Port Said. We were assembled in a long line and our names were read out, to which we had to answer 'Here' in succession. When it came to Iain's turn, a piping voice answered, 'Here.' In response to the Colonel's 'Who are you?' – the voice answered, 'I am Lieutenant Moncreiffe's orderly, sent on the toughening-up course instead of him.'

There was considerable shelling along the River Garigliano as the German observation posts overlooked our positions from the lower slopes of the Aurunci mountains on the other side. But we were too far away for accuracy as we were entrenched a mile back from the river bank. German patrols, however, sometimes crossed in rubber boats after dark. There was a scare one night when one of our dispatch riders was shot dead on his motor cycle just beside Battalion Headquarters.

On Christmas Eve I was sent out on standing patrol among the floods near the river's edge to see if this was a route that the German patrols were using. It was a wild night with flurries of sleet blowing in our faces as we crouched along the edge of the river. Round us the floodwaters were alive with wildfowl, splashing and quacking continuously despite the fury of the elements. Sometimes the duck would start a loud splashing and quacking as we all faced towards them with fingers on the trigger. But no Germans came our way.

A standing patrol was also maintained at the river's mouth to protect an artillery observation post there among some scattered houses called Puntafiume; but a German contingent crossed in rubber boats one night and dislodged them. The recapture of Puntafiume was therefore planned for a few nights later in conjunction with a commando raid round the river mouth to test the German defences preparatory to the future crossing of the river. Two platoons of Right Flank were attached to 'F' Company for this operation. My orders were to recapture Puntafiume itself while 'F' Company were to secure a portion of the riverbank to the east. The commandos were to land from assault craft on the north side of the river, mop up German outposts in their neighbourhood and then retire through our bridgehead at dawn. We were not to withdraw to our old positions until the last of the commandos had returned.

Under cover of an artillery barrage my platoon re-occupied the battered houses of Puntafiume without any opposition. From the German side of the river Verey lights were now fired over our heads to illuminate the long lines of 'F' Company on our right crouching along the floodbank. Seeing where we were, the enemy then opened fire with mortars and caused several casualties as none of us were dug in. Nor could we fire back with mortars or artillery as the commandos were supposed to be coming in from the sea and we had instructions on no account to fire across the river for fear of hitting them. Actually their nearest unit had got stuck on a sandbank on the wrong side of the river mouth and it was only later in the night that the rest landed further north along the beaches to outflank the enemy in a surprise attack. Amidst the resultant Spandau and Bren gun fire we suddenly heard the skirl of their bagpipes playing, by coincidence, my own company's march. This stirring pibroch, sounding out across the marshes, called to the eternal clansman in us all. It is the only musical instrument still played in battle.

By dawn the commandos had retired according to plan, bringing not only some German prisoners with their wounded, but also some six corpses of their own, blown up on a minefield. Despite this minefield they had nevertheless achieved all their objectives in this so-called 'reconnaissance by force'.

Apart from having my field telephone link with 'F' Company Headquarters repeatedly cut by mortar fire (and bravely mended each time by a signaller) my platoon had spent a not uncomfortable night at Puntafiume. As dawn broke, however, 'F' Company withdrew according to plan: but I was required under commanding officer's orders to remain where I was with my platoon to ensure that every single commando had already returned safely across the river. But how could one know this? When it was broad daylight and the expected order to withdraw to our own lines did not arrive, I grew more and more perturbed. Here were the best part of two infantry companies ranged along the open river bank and not dug in (for we carried no spades) right under the Germans' noses. It was at least half an hour since the last commando had returned and now broad daylight; but still no order came to withdraw. Battalion Head-quarters had a command carrier about a quarter of a mile behind – also in full view of the enemy – and my Commanding Officer was attempting to get the new Brigadier's permission to withdraw. This he was reluctant to give thinking there might still be some stray commandos on the other side. But it was now long past the pre-arranged time for withdrawal and I felt a hornets' nest on the German side might be expected to erupt at any moment. I knew there was a main road there along which the Germans had recently been running lorries mounted with multi-barrelled Nebelwerfer mortars.

My platoon signaller kept sending messages to the command carrier: 'Hello Roger, hello Roger, have you any message for us? Over.' 'Hello Easy, hello Easy, sorry no message yet. Out.' Mutters of 'What are the something bastards up to?' At last our wireless crackled into life with the Commanding Officer's codeword for permission to withdraw. It transpired that he had finally taken it upon himself to give the order to retire without reference to the Brigadier.

As prearranged, I took my platoon at the run through the open fields behind; we maintained disciplined order, spread out in three lines with everyone ten yards apart. After about 300 yards we slowed to a walking pace. Immediately afterwards I had the satisfaction of looking back and seeing the whole of Puntafiume and the south bank of the river behind us erupting like a volcano as all the German artillery and Nebelwerfers ranged on the floodbank where we had just been lying out in the open. The bombardment was still proceed-ing as we reached our former lines and passed a white-faced Brigadier accompanied by one of his intelligence officers. He asked me in trepidation how many casualties I had sustained, to which I was able curtly to reply 'Not a single one', and walked on past him without a further word.

We then reoccupied our old positions while the commandos boarded a fleet of lorries waiting to convey them back to Sorrento where they had been training for this operation for the last few months. Blankets were draped over them by waiting attendants and they were served with rum and hot breakfasts from NAAFI vans while press photographers took their photographs. As the lorries drove off, there was much genial banter from our guardsmen at the expense of these 'Movie Men'.

On New Year's Eve we handed over to another brigade and marched back to a base area where the Italian population were very hostile, having recently been indiscriminately bombed by the Allies when they were still behind the German lines. Our Special Investigation Department had discovered that our dispatch rider shot outside battalion headquarters had been shot not by a German patrol, but by a local Fascist. The only Italians in this area who appeared to be on our side were Communists.

I spent the afternoon of New Year's day shooting duck. All local fowling pieces had, as a precautionary measure, been ordered by Military Government to be handed in to the *carabinieri*; so we were able to arm ourselves with a selection of old Italian 16-bores and hammer guns. Armed with these, I and the Adjutant, together with 'Feathers', who was now Second-in-Command of the Battalion, and Frank Waldron, our anti-tank gun platoon commander, set off into no man's land to shoot wildfowl for our New Year dinner.

Incongruously garbed in fur jackets and I wearing my Alpini hat from Capri, we made our way through the forward lines now manned by the Cheshire Regiment to the point in no man's land near where I had already vainly tried to shoot duck with Bren guns.

German shell fire had by now grown noticeably less and it seemed unlikely that German patrols would disturb us – at least not so early in the evening. My stance was behind a hedge near the Garigliano. As it grew dark the duck started flighting in hundreds from the sea – so many that all could not be fired at and scores kept landing with splashes in the water at our feet. My cartridges kept on jamming and finally one completely jammed my left-hand barrel so I was left firing only with the right. Even so I managed to bag seven duck. When it was almost dark and I was again wrestling with jammed cartridges, three men suddenly leapt out of the hedge at me brandishing machine-pistols. For one awful moment I thought I had been captured again. But they turned out to be a patrol from the neighbouring battalion sent out to discover what all the shooting was about. I was able to placate their sergeant with a brace of duck. We would have been able to retrieve many more had we had dogs; but, even so, our total pick was twenty duck – not bad going right under the Germans' noses.

Unfortunately the shooting had been too much for our opponents and according to the complaint later received through Divisional Headquarters, a barrage had then descended on our successors, the Cheshires, immediately after our departure. They were justifiably incensed at the Guards waiting until they were out of the line before hotting up their front by duck-shooting. Actually our new Commanding Officer could not afford to be too angry because he knew beforehand of our intentions. He also ate some of the duck at our overdue Christmas party which took place a few days later when the Battalion had moved back to Aversa.

This Battalion 'smoker' was a party to end all parties. Major General Templer, commanding the 56th Division, was our guest of honour, together with the Brigadier, in the officers' mess. Then all repaired to the sergeants' mess where, after an hour's hard drinking and speechifying, things began to get boisterous. So much so that when Sergeant-Major Lumsden sat down beside the General and started to give him his intoxicated views on his division, both he and the General had to be discreetly removed. Lieutenant-Quartermaster Greenwood, who had been with 2SG all the whole way from Egypt tried to make a speech about the Battalion's long record, but no one could hear what he was trying to say.

I left just before the end when things looked like getting really out of hand. Missiles were flying in all directions and the Regimental Sergeant-Major was running about putting his cap on at intervals to look official and so restore order, and then taking if off again and joining in the general mêlée.

Life out of the line, however, was not really a riot of parties: there was also the normal round of drill parades, weapon and kit inspections and tactical training. Colonel 'Boy' Harris, our new Commanding Officer from the disbanded 4th Battalion, was obviously beginning to realise that the Battalion had a great fighting spirit behind its facade of battle weariness; but he still deemed it his duty to give us a 'straight from the shoulder' talk about the things he thought were wrong. One of these, which had substance, was the reform of Support Company.

He said they were to stop living in the aura of Medenine and to cease brewing up tea the whole time. In particular, the anti-tank platoon (the heroes of Medenine but for whom no role could be found in this mountain terrain) were to have an assault course planned for them over which they could practise manhandling their guns. The very idea of these heroes doing any such thing thrilled the rest of us.

There was no doubt, however, that out of the line the Battalion did benefit from some discipline and pulling together. There was also now quite an officer problem as so many had been lost since the Salerno landings; but Colonel Boy's handling of the officer situation was unfortunate, although he was always friendly to me. He set about removing our Adjutant, who was a personal friend, in a rather unpleasant way. He asked him, as if conferring a favour, to command the carrier platoon. This would have been a clear demotion, as he had already commanded that platoon with distinction in North Africa. Colonel Boy may have been entitled to his own 4th Battalion Adjutant; but that was hardly the way to go about it. Anthony Balfour, who had just commanded Right Flank with distinction at Rocchetta, was told that he was being transferred elsewhere as he was not wanted as a company commander. Colonel Boy, however, was somewhat embarrassed when, only a few days later, he had to congratulate Tony on his award of the Military Cross for the Rocchetta affair. Tony told me ruefully that Colonel Boy had then said smoothly, 'My dear Tony, I always knew you were a good soldier.'

Shortly afterwards both he and the Adjutant were snapped up by our 1st Battalion now preparing for the Anzio landings. They were both killed at Anzio commanding companies during the next month's fighting, which was a great loss – experienced commanders were now becoming few and far between. Colonel Guy Taylor, transferred after Rocchetta, was also killed while commanding the 1st Battalion later in the Italian campaign.

Quite a number of other 4th Battalion officers were also inserted into 2SG at this juncture. Colonel Boy decided that it was about time our middle-aged signals officer (a former London stockbroker) who had been most of the way through North Africa should be replaced by a younger ex-4th Battalion subaltern. He was a favourite with the men and could always be calculated to extract humour out of every situation. The night before he was due to leave, his guardsmen gave him a great send-off at the end of which they wheeled him home in a wheelbarrow. Next day he was much too fragile to move; and also

[93]

the day after. Thereafter he just stayed on with his new 4th Battalion substitute but now as his junior officer.

Colonel Boy now wisely abandoned the idea of trying to rid himself of all the old 2SG characters and turn the Battalion into a faded image of his disbanded 4th Battalion. It was 'they' who each had to become one of 'us'.

There were also one or two 3rd Battalion officers (although no guardsmen) now transferred from the tank battalion of the Regiment which already had enough reserve officers in England. These ex-tank officers proved readily adaptable to infantry fighting and indeed 'F' Company was commanded by one of them.

Right Flank was fortunate to have as its new commander Major Digby Raeburn, who had served in the Battalion during the early days in North Africa but had since been a full colonel on the Cairo staff. He now took demotion in favour of active service and quickly gained the firm respect of us all. The newcomers all came, in due course, to assimilate the outlook and traditions of the older men. In particular our able new Adjutant from the 4th Battalion very soon became one of us.

The Garigliano river was now successfully crossed by the 46th and 56th Divisions to establish a new line along the foothills on the other side; but still overlooked by the enemy entrenched on the foothills of the Arunci mountains. There the rival entrenchments were only a short distance apart. The Battalion took over a section of our line in January 1944 beside the hilltop town of Minturno.

One night the Germans fired a new rocket device at our positions, which was the prototype of the 'Flying Bombs' about to be fired on London. Sergeant 'Joe Plush' Wilson christened this the 'Horror Gun'. It came over, as he described it, 'with full headlights on and landed with a screech of brakes'. The subsequent underground explosions caused a 70-foot crater and tons of mud clattering down around us in the middle of the night with a noise like a cavalry charge. However, no one was killed.

We occupied positions in this area for about six weeks. On average this meant seven days in the line followed by three days' rest. Being in the line was not just a fight against the enemy, but more against the grim monotony of perpetual pouring rain, and constant shelling. Some sections were down to four men and the problem of posting double sentries at night – and then expecting the men to be fit for patrols as well – became acute. But one hardly ever saw a German.

Mount Natale on the west flank was the worst location. There was a deluge of rain when we took over there at night from the Cameronians. Their slit trenches on a forward slope had become filled to the top with water, so they were simply standing in the darkness beside them when we arrived. We baled out these two-man slit trenches all through the night with our mess tins or steel helmets, for we had to stay underground all day as we were under observation on a forward slope. For some unaccountable reason I was forbidden to move back on to the reverse slope. The mud was so sodden that our slit trenches soon filled up again, while we sat on branches suspended halfway up the sides. The snow only came in the form of sleet although the mountain tops in front were now covered in a white mantle. I spent three days like this, soaked to the skin. It seemed worse than the 1914–18 war when deep trenches were all interconnected and there were also communal dug-outs.

On the third night the Germans brought up a mortar to fire harassing shots at my platoon, which they must have observed on our forward slope. Their shooting was very accurate, as they put down over thirty bombs on one of my section positions. But fortunately only half of them exploded in the deep mud. Two bombs landed near me in the same slit trench as two guardsmen. The first broke one man's leg and the next bomb blew the other's head off. I was glad the night was dark when I removed what remained of one man in order to get the survivor on to a stretcher. He was very brave about it and kept on telling the stretcher-bearers to leave him and take cover in a slit-trench until the mortaring was over. Our stretcher-bearers were always outstanding. To our right York and Lancasters were driven off Mount Natale by the only German counter-attack.

I was amazed at the tenacity of the Italian civilians marooned in no man's land, who did not leave their homes even under intense shell fire. Understandably they did not favour either side. One day three girls were wounded by 88 mm fire in the adjoining house to our 'rest' billets where my platoon periodically retired. I had them carried to the ground floor of an adjoining nunnery and into a room where I could see some fifty wounded civilians for whom the medical aid was quite inadequate. I put the most severely wounded girl on our company jeep (fitted for stretchers) to convey her to the MO's tent; but she screamed at the prospect of leaving her relations. All the nuns then came out and screamed as well. We removed her all the same as she would otherwise have died. The nuns had already buried six casualties under the paving-stones of their nunnery garden, which was holy ground. But they had not buried them effectively and the air was fetid.

Allied Military Government were now trying to evacuate all these civilians from the Allied bridgehead north of the Garigliano. As agricultural peasants, however, they were loath to leave their few acres. I saw an old man ploughing in front of Mount Natale while a battle was in progress. He wore a long black cloak and seemed impervious to the shellfire. Eventually, because of heavy casualties, the Allied Military Government forced the evacuation of the whole population of the little town of Minturno that was now in the middle of no man's land. This led to its wholesale looting by those of our troops who had motor transport. But this did not include the infantry companies.

One of the many duties of a platoon officer in the front line was censoring guardsmen's letters for breaches of security. This unpleasant task, however, gave a good pointer to their morale. Mostly they were cheerful under the most appalling conditions. They scribbled away endlessly whenever the sun came out and I suppose the Germans did so on the other side. There were a series of intricate abbreviations one needed to know. ITALY was short for 'I trust and love you'. On the envelope flap often appeared SWALK – 'Sealed with a loving kiss'. I wondered what SWOS meant till I was told by my orderly that this meant 'Sealed with officer's saliva'. BURMA was another appearing on a letter to the wife. It stood for 'Be Upstairs Ready My Angel'!

We were three solid weeks in our final position on Mount Tufo waiting for an American division to take over. By that time half of us were lousy and had to be deloused in a mobile bath unit just behind the line.

It still rained or snowed most of the time. At night we laboured to erect barbed wire fences along the crest of the hill. Then the engineers came and laid 'S' mines in front of us, which had an uncanny knack of exploding during the heavy rain, causing everyone to 'stand to' in the soaking darkness. There were also reconnaissance and standing patrols from which one returned wet to the skin. With no house or fire to return to, one simply stripped to one's dripping underclothes, rolled oneself in a couple of dry blankets and tried to sleep. We had ground-sheets over the top; but when the terrace above reached saturation point the trench was apt to fill suddenly with water in the space of a minute.

It was a grim existence, but there were lighter moments to be

The author

The Battalion about to leave for Italy, 1943. The author is seated front row on right.

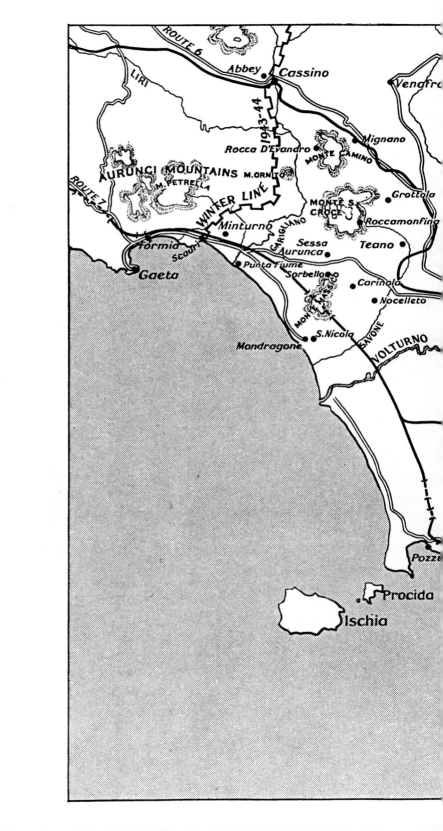

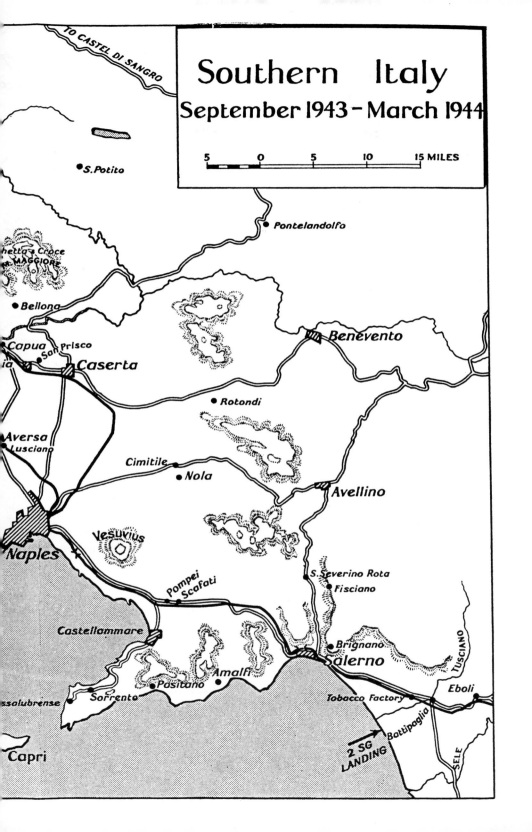

Southern Italy
September 1943 – March 1944

5   0   5   10   15 MILES

TO CASTEL DI SANGRO

S. Potito

Pontelandolfo

hetta Croce
M. MAGGIORE

Bellona

Capua
Prisco
San
Caserta
ia

Benevento

Rotondi

Aversa
Lusciano

Cimitile
Nola

Avellino

Vesuvius

S. Severino Rota
Fisciano

Naples

Pompei
Scafati

Castellammare

Brignano
Salerno

Amalfi

TUSCIANO

Pasitano

Eboli

ssolubrense
Sorrento

Tobacco Factory

Battipaglia

Capri

2 SG
LANDING

SELE

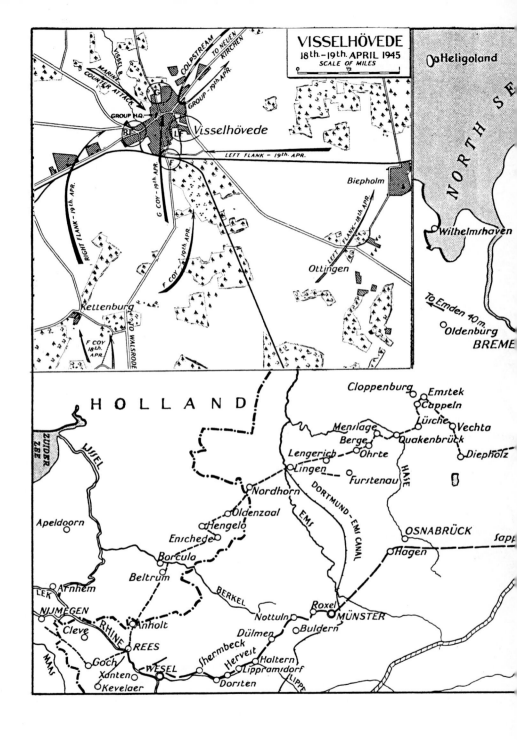

VISSELHÖVEDE
18th–19th. APRIL 1945
SCALE OF MILES
½

VISSEL B.

COLDSTREAM TO NEUEN KIRCHEN

MARINE COUNTER ATTACK

GROUP – 19th. APR.

GROUP H.Q.

RE.

L.

Visselhövede

LEFT FLANK – 19th. APR.

RIGHT FLANK – 19th. APR.

G COY – 19th. APR.

F COY – 19th. APR.

TO WALSRODE

Kettenburg

F COY 18th. APR.

Biepholm

LEFT FLANK – 18th. APR.

Ottingen

HELIGOLAND

NORTH SEA

Wilhelmshaven

To Emden 40m.

Oldenburg

BREME

H O L L A N D

ZUIDER ZEE

IJSEL

LEK

Apeldoorn

Arnhem

NIJMEGEN

Cleve

RHINE

MAAS

Goch

REES

Xanten

Kevelaer

WESEL

Dorsten

Hervest

Lippramsdorf

Schermbeck

LIPPE

Haltern

Dülmen

Buldern

Nottuln

Roxel

MÜNSTER

BERKEL

Beltrum

Borcula

Enschede

Hengelo

Oldenzaal

Nordhorn

Lingen

Lengerich

Furstenau

EMS

DORTMUND – EMS CANAL

HASE

Hagen

OSNABRÜCK

Sapp

Ohrte

Berge

Menslage

Quakenbrück

Diepholz

Lüsche

Vechta

Cappeln

Emstek

Cloppenburg

Anholt

FROM THE RHINE
TO THE BALTIC

0   10   20   30   40 MILES

━━━━━━━━━ ···········Autobahn

- - - - - - - - ··········Route of 2nd. Bn.

— — — — — ·········Route of 3rd. Bn.

Lieutenant-Colonel Taylor inspecting 2nd Battalion NCOs in Salerno Stadium, 30 September 1943. Behind him are Major Steuart-Fothringham and the Adjutant, Captain Weir.

remembered. There was laughter when the rain stopped and the sun went down in a blaze of glory behind the Gulf of Gaeta. Then the olive groves, stretching in terraces up the mountain side, turned from gold to grey and then to jet black. Sometimes too there was a golden dawn after it had been raining all night and my platoon reappeared in blankets, laughing and joking as they dried themselves out by a roaring fire.

There was a stone hut for storing grapes in my area and we used to brew tea there for the platoon. Tea was a social affair presided over by myself and Sergeant Macphee, the chief delicacy being globe artichokes which we put on to boil and ate with melted butter. We frequently had various members of the 3-inch mortar platoon from down the slope as guests. Corporal Bryson used also to come over and give us what he called his 'morale brew' which concluded with his views on sex, religion and politics. He was now in charge of the company snipers. At night he used to take a swig at his 'horror bottle', pick up a couple of grenades and then go out with one or two other men. As one of them told me, they used to proceed as stealthily as mice skirting the German minefields till suddenly Corporal Bryson would bellow at them at the top of his voice not to 'make a noise like a herd of bloody elephants' and then disappear on his own, crashing unscathed through the undergrowth. Most afternoons he used to go out and try to catch 'old Gallene', which was the name he gave to a scraggy old Italian hen which lived in the ruins of a shelled house, well down the forward slope. This was unpopular as his presence led to shelling; but he was determined to catch 'old Gallene' if it was the last thing he did. It was indeed. A concentration of shells came down and he was hit by a small fragment in the back of the neck. We could hear his Falstaffian laughter echoing round the company position as he pulled out the shrapnel shouting, 'You bastard, sir!' at the Germans. A minute later another shell landed and killed him.

There was a lot of shelling next day, as the Germans now appeared to have Battalion Headquarters itself well registered. They had the advantage, so far as artillery ranging fire was concerned, of having themselves occupied this area before and of knowing where our command positions were likely to be. A sudden concentration of shelling killed Colonel Boy Harris and also wounded the medical officer. I had two casualties as we were dug in just above; so we moved to alternative positions – which was just as well as one shell landed on the very slit trench I had just vacated.

At the beginning of March we were informed that we were to be relieved by an American infantry division and that 201 Guards Brigade, being short of reinforcements, was being sent home to be regrouped for the expected Second Front. All guardsmen still serving in the Battalion who had fought in the Middle East now left for Naples at long last to board the 'the ship with the tartan funnel'. They numbered 141. It was indeed scandalous that married men who had been abroad since 1939 had not been allowed home at the end of the Desert Campaign. But a drawback of the regimental system was that it lacked authority in such respects.

I also hoped to squeeze in on the long-awaited 'ship with the tartan funnel' rather than be transferred to the 1st Battalion. The future prospect of eventually fighting on the Western Front was outweighed by that of going home and remaining with the battalion to which I felt I belonged.

Our relieving force was the American 88th Division straight from the USA. Their 'key personnel' came to live with us in the front line before taking over. For the occasion, and to deceive the enemy, they had been made to wear British steel helmets. They regarded these as extremely funny and, unlike their own, impossible to use for brewing up tea. They lived with us in the front line for about a week and were excellent companions. We swapped our rum ration for their cigars – although they were strictly not allowed to drink in the front line. We, however, got a rum ration if conditions were really bad.

Their military organisation was notably different from our own and modelled more upon that of the Germans. They had about forty-five men to an infantry platoon whereas we were now down to half that number. But their supporting field artillery, like that of the Germans, was only half of ours and they had nothing to compare with our defensive artillery barrages in the event of German attack.

I shared my dug-out with my relief American platoon officer. One night I had to take out a patrol to try to locate German movements or minefields in front. He asked if he could accompany me with some of his men. They were all very keen and argued among themselves as to who was to come; so that in the end far too many of them insisted on joining the patrol. This Anglo-American herd then trampled off into the darkness making such an appalling noise that I soon withdrew the lot. My American opposite number turned out to be a German called Muller whose parents had become naturalised Americans. He said his uncles still lived in Germany and for all he knew his cousins might be in the Wehrmacht. He even spoke American with a German accent. Another American officer called Murphy was of Irish descent; his directions always appeared to be overruled by his platoon sergeant. He wore two German revolvers purchased from us.

I'll never forget the last shell. It was while we were waiting next evening with our American friends for the rest of their battalion to arrive. It was pouring with rain as usual but there had not been a shell all afternoon; so we were sheltering in a small barn. Suddenly it came out of the night, a single shell screeching like the devil through the darkness and landed in a shower of sparks fifty feet below. I could almost hear Corporal Bryson's ghostly laughter. We waited a long time for the final contingent of American GIs to arrive. Their approach was heralded by the voice of Benson, our company runner, guiding them up the hill. We could hear him 'swinging it' on the Americans: he had been in Right Flank since the original Battle of Sollum.

We then drove all night along the coast road, through Naples to Sorrento, where we moved into company billets in a large villa on a cliff top above 'Poppa's Restaurant'. From here one could gaze straight across the bay to Mount Vesuvius which had just stopped smoking as the rim of its crater had collapsed, blocking the vent.

Next day we scrubbed our equipment white, discarded our stocking caps, and replaced them with smart service dress ones. Every morning resounded to the tramp of feet marching to and fro across the town square to the amazement of the local Italians. The Regimental Sergeant-Major now at last came into his own. It was surprising how smart the old veterans could be in comparison to my last recollection of them at Minturno, in dirty stocking caps crouched over an old brew can.

A few nights later we were driving back in the early hours over the mountain road after a party at Positano – reached now by a new Bailey bridge where the former bridge had been blown. As we topped the crest to drive down to Sorrento we were suddenly confronted by the awesome splendour of Mount Vesuvius in full (and as it turned out final) eruption. It had literally just blown its top. The whole sky above Naples was lit up and jagged tongues of flaming lava poured down the mountainside. Even at fifteen miles' range one could hear the incessant roar like some primeval bellows.

Next morning Vesuvius exuded a massive pillar of smoke rising to 1,500 feet, scattering a dense cloud of lava in all directions and (as we later heard) destroying between thirty and forty American fighter planes on a nearby airfield. As picquet officer I had to call off the morning's drill parade as the Regimental Sergeant-Major became more and more hoarse and was finally choked into silence by the lava dust now lying six inches deep. This was how the town of Pompeii must have been engulfed in the first century A.D. The local Italians said that it was the Wrath of God for the current destruction of Italy by the Allies.

I took my platoon next day in two closed 3-ton lorries up the circuitous road on Vesuvius to the meteorological station situated on top. The lava was only flowing down two sides of the mountain and our 3-tonners made such a noise ascending the steep gradient we could not hear the volcano itself. But when we finally stopped at the station near the summit the noise from just above our heads was deafening. The top of the volcano appeared to explode every thirty seconds in gigantic pink and purple clouds which mushroomed to a height of several thousand feet. Large lumps of pumice stone kept landing around us so that we all quickly dived back into the lorries and drove back down the mountain at full speed. Near the bottom we observed the slow moving lava or clinkers engulfing the village of San Sebastian. A church or a house would burst into flame as the thirty-foot wall hemmed it round. Then it would totter, and crumble with the overpowering weight.

Waiting for the troopships to take us home we used to spend our weekends on the other side of the peninsula. From Amalfi on a clear day one could see 'Roger' and 'Sugar' beaches at Salerno; but mostly they were hidden in the mists. Since landing there in September 1943 the Battalion had lost 20 officers and 147 guardsmen killed and 23 officers and 286 guardsmen wounded, as well as 82 reported missing. We now had to say goodbye to the new additions to the Battalion who were understandably transferred to the 1st Battalion which was suffering heavy casualties in the Anzio Bridgehead.

All our old battered trucks and carriers from North Africa were now sent away – some still with their 'Desert Rat' emblazonings. But we still had seven jeeps, surplus to establishments concealed by Support Company in the orange groves. Some of this company also still wore their black berets, Hebron sheepskin coats and suede desert boots to show where their old loyalties still lay.

Just before the Battalion sailed for home we were visited at Sorrento by General Sir Oliver Leese, a Coldstreamer, now commanding the 8th Army, who came to say goodbye. He made a speech to all ranks in which he said that he had heard of our exploits in Italy and he might hear about us again in North-West Europe. But he added that from henceforth the Germans knew they were beaten and no attack would be launched without complete air and artillery superiority. Nevertheless one had to look back to earlier days for the true tests of endurance.

7

Back to Training

The sea sparkled and glided endlessly backwards from our large convoy of troopships. The convoy carried not only British troops but
also men of the American 82nd Airborne Division, also bound for the
Second Front having played a leading part at Salerno in holding the
American bridgehead. The days glided by as swiftly as the sea. We
passed Cape Bon where the sand looked strangely orange after the
mud of Italy. Off the Spanish coast there was a huge flock of migrat-
ing flamingos which glinted pink and scarlet as they wheeled and
circled in the sunlight. Then we skirted the west coast of Ireland with
the rain coming down in squalls and finally were back in Liverpool.
We landed there at the same quay from which we had started a year
and a half before. It was still drizzling.

At seven o'clock next morning we were on a London railway plat-
form with the regimental pipers playing the regimental march and a
galaxy of red tabs to welcome the Battalion home after an absence
overseas of no less than five years. Next day being Sunday we attended a service of thanksgiving in the chapel of Wellington Barracks
where we were billeted. Over the altar were emblazoned the words
'Be thou faithful unto death, and I will give thee a crown of life.'

Alastair Erskine and I, who had both landed at Salerno, were
chosen as platoon officers to mount a special King's Guard (in khaki
battledress) at Buckingham Palace. But we were not allowed to do so
with our webbing equipment blancoed white in 8th Army fashion,
nor with the regimental band, as requested, playing the adopted
German tune of 'Lilli Marlene'.

Shortly afterwards the skeleton Battalion and a skeleton 201
Guards Brigade HQ moved north to Stobs Camp in Scotland on a
bleak moor near Hawick. I joined them there at the beginning of June
1944, after a short bout of jaundice. Here the Battalion was to be
made up to strength again for the impending Second Front.

This hutted camp had originally been built to house German
prisoners during the 1914–18 war. It may have been habitable enough

then; but now, due to lack of subsequent maintenance, the wind whistled through it and the huts were crawling with rats which we tried to exterminate with smoke bombs. We thought this a bit thick after so long abroad. However, the locals were very hospitable, the camp was in some attractive border country, and I could also get home for occasional weekends.

201 Guards Brigade was now purely a training brigade. The Battalion was to be brought up to war strength again, and then re-trained as motorised infantry for the Guards Armoured Division. The latter had already landed in Normandy as part of the Second Front which opened in May 1944. Promotions in the skeleton Battalion were rapid for many of the seasoned guardsmen who had come home from Italy. They were mainly Scottish as the Regiment had most of its recruiting offices in Scotland. A succession of NCOs' cadre courses were run in drill and weapon training for those who would now be training all the new recruits expected to arrive shortly to bring the Battalion up to battle strength again.

I was still a platoon officer, which might seem strange being one of only four subalterns still surviving from Salerno. None of us, however, were promoted; for promotion within the Regiment did not work that way. The replacement of officer casualties was usually on the basis of seniority. Thus all our new company commanders were regular officers of many years' service, two of whom had been colonels on staff jobs and had now reverted to their regimental rank of major in order to see active service. All four company commanders were indeed outstanding soldiers of considerable battle experience. We also had a popular new commanding officer in Colonel Henry Clowes.

It was galling, nevertheless, for a young officer like myself to see new captains set over him – thus dampening his hopes of promotion and incidentally of survival. But so it was.

With a complete complement again of thirty officers and a cadre of battle-experienced non-commissioned officers under them, we awaited our new 'guardsmen' recruits. Normally such would have come from the Guards Depot – but there were none left there. We had already heard disquieting rumours about where our recruits were to come from. The Guards Depot where all guardsmen received their initial training in drill and discipline had already been denuded in supplying reinforcements for the depleted 201 Guards Brigade; the 1st Guards Brigade which had suffered similar casualties at Anzio; and also for the 6th Guards Tank Brigade now fighting in Normandy.

Guardsmen in tanks, however, were a completely new phenomenon. When German panzers broke through a gap in the French Maginot Line in 1940 causing the collapse of France and the eventual withdrawal of the British Expeditionary Force, it was decided by the War Office that equivalent British panzers should be created. Hence the Brigade of Guards should have its own 'panzer' units with selected guardsmen still undergoing only their initial training in discipline and turnout at the Guards Depot. Thereafter, those of higher IQ (as revealed by IQ tests) were to receive separate tank training in the Sherman tanks of the Guards Armoured Division, or in the Churchill tanks of the 6th Independent Guards Tank Brigade which contained the 3rd Battalion Scots Guards. That the latter were riding in British-made Churchill tanks named after the Prime Minister himself appears to have been a vital factor in stopping the 3rd Battalion losing its tanks and having all its guardsmen transferred to the 2nd Battalion. So new infantrymen had now to be quickly found for the 2nd Battalion.

On 10 June 1944 400 RAF reinforcements accordingly arrived off a train at Hawick still wearing their sky blue uniforms. These aircraftsmen had mainly been guarding aerodromes and were no longer needed in that role. Most were anti-Army and anti-Brigade of Guards in particular, so they marched up the hill to our camp chanting, 'We are the RAF, RAF, RAF!' 201 Guards Brigade thus received some 1,500 men of the disbanded RAF Regiment and the Battalion in particular about 400 to make us up to strength again for the invasion of Europe.

This then posed the serious problem of how to attract a new sense of loyalty among these RAF Regiment newcomers who already had a different RAF allegiance of their own. It involved the eradication of one identity and the substitution of another. And such a transformation had now to be achieved in a very short space of time.

The Brigadier had rightly stipulated that, before this could be effected, a brand new parade ground of rolled tarmac be constructed in the middle of this ex-prisoner-of-war camp. In short it had to be transformed into a mini-Guards Depot. On arrival the new recruits had their blue uniforms whisked off them and replaced by khaki battledress. They were then pounced upon by the Battalion drill sergeants as a bunch of RAF riff-raff and for several weeks were paraded up and down in drill formations by platoons and companies until they could hold themselves erect, take some pride in their new appearance and conduct basic drill movements in unison. The emphasis was on smartness and turn-out under the direction of RSM Barnstaple, who was a complete martinet.

By drilling soldiers into a sense of uniformity, the members of each unit come physically to act and perceive themselves on parade to be acting as one man. The suggestive patter of the drill sergeants was incessant. The first ten minutes of each drill period were expended in 'warming up' or 'chasing' in double quick time – left turn, right turn, about turn, halt! – and woe betide the man who ended up facing in the wrong direction. Some of the new recruits simply could not take all this 'chasing', although others, seeing its purpose, later retracted their requests for transfer. Real misfits, nevertheless, were allowed to be transferred. But gradually a growing sense of uniformity began to emerge and to outweigh the fear of retribution, on which less emphasis now needed to be placed.

Every British regiment has its own peculiarities of drill. When some individual made a wrong movement he would be snarled at and told he was not in the 'bloody so and so's'. A great deal of this patter ('bullshit' in army parlance) was purposely humorous. During the panting intervals of 'stand easy', regimental history questions were fired at the new recruits until they knew that the Regiment was founded in Scotland in 1642, became a Royal Guard in 1660 and was later moved to London as the 3rd (later the Scots) Guards. There was particular emphasis on the tradition and battle honours of the Regiment. Then there was the enforced saluting (symbolic of obedience) of officers who had to salute back in return. All this 'bullshit' not only involved the crude enforcement of homogeneity within the Regiment (which most had never heard of before) but also a healthy prejudice against outsiders. Nicknames of others abounded and the Germans were referred to as 'Jerries' or 'Krauts'.

A full battalion parade was the most important occasion for inducing group identity or *esprit de corps*. The parade ground was sacred territory across which every man had to march properly to attention. On battalion parade too the new recruits were able to see where they fitted into the military structure of platoons and companies and who their officers were. This was therefore identity-formation as seen on parade, with each sub-unit sufficiently small for each man to know where he belonged.

The RAF aircraftsmen were thus gradually induced to identify as Scots Guardsmen belonging to different units of its 2nd Battalion or

2SG. All platoons had numbers and the company names remained as Left Flank, 'F' Company, 'G' Company and Right Flank. The recruits soon began to identify with their platoon numbers and the name or letter of their company. They were also beginning to identify not only as Scots Guardsmen but also as 2nd Battalion men.

Most of them took all this 'bullshit' remarkably well despite being given absolute hell for the first two or three weeks. But they were nevertheless well looked after. There was an officer to every thirty men instructed to get to know each one individually, their home life and personal problems. A particular bone of contention, however, was that by being conscripted from the RAF Regiment into the PBI (Poor Bloody Infantry) they had lost an extra 6d a day of pay for the so-called skilled work of guarding aerodromes against German parachutists who never appeared. After negotiation with the Air Ministry it was agreed to make up this deficiency, but to the understandable annoyance of our veterans.

A 'chasing' on the parade ground was certainly one way of weeding out the old crocks who would not have made good soldiers in action. About five per cent of the new recruits could not 'take it' and fell out after the first week – being mainly the very young or middle-aged. It was better to find this out at the start. Most however knew that there were only four months left before going into action; and having been warned what to expect, were on their mettle. They had spent the war so far in boring jobs on aerodromes and were now keen to 'have a crack at the Hun'. There next ensued an extensive period of weapon training on the ranges using rifles and automatic Bren guns; but still keeping up the occasional drill parade.

To mark the end of this training period the whole Battalion, on 24 September 1944, attended a memorial service in St Giles Cathedral, Edinburgh, combined with the laying up of a set of 2SG's old colours. Right Flank provided the escort. After the service and an inspection by the Colonel of the Regiment, the Duke of Gloucester, the whole Battalion marched behind the pipes and drums down Princes Street where His Royal Highness took the salute. The newspapers commented on our fine appearance but would hardly have believed that only four months before we had been but a skeleton battalion and now over half the men were ex-RAF Regiment.

As we now had only two months left before going into action, our time was to be spent on training, first on a platoon, then on a company, and finally on a whole battalion basis.

For this period of tactical training, Alastair Erskine and I, as experienced platoon officers, were seconded to an attached company of the Coldstream Guards which had also been made up to strength, again with ex-RAF Regiment recruits. We were billeted for this purpose in Bowhill House near Selkirk, where the surrounding hills provided an ideal training ground. We also had attached to us a Norwegian artillery battery for firing live artillery barrages and getting us used to advancing in line behind them. A number of Border sheep were killed in the process but fortunately no humans.

None of this live training, however, appeared to apply to the old soaks of Support Company (the heroes of Medenine) with their 6-pounder anti-tank guns, 3-inch mortars and Bren gun carriers that had hardly been used in Italy. They had more 'five year men' than any other company and thus needed no RAF Regiment recruits to bring them up to strength again. As Frank Waldron put it on one occasion, Support Company only joined in these training exercises for the instruction of the new Commanding Officer!

8

The German Frontier

The Battalion left Stobs Camp on 27 January 1945 deep in snow. One of our 6-pounder anti-tank guns slid down a slope and crashed into the wall of the officers' mess. We then ploughed our way on foot through ten inches of snow to Hawick railway station, looking more like the remnants of Napoleon's Grand Army retreating from Moscow than 2SG returning to the fray. By the time the train was due to leave our anti-tank guns were still bogged down but this did not matter much as the engine driver and fireman had both gone on strike. Another driver was eventually found. The train started and we rattled southwards through the night, reaching Purfleet station near Tilbury at 3.45 a.m. next morning. There did not seem to be anyone about who knew where we should go; but Drill-Sergeant Fraser's voice could awaken the dead and there was soon a host of guides, leading us in all directions.

We spent three days on a transport landing ship whose naval crew were very hospitable. It had the motto 'Semper Pongo's' painted on it which caused much banter, as also some self-styled 'battle honours' which surprisingly included 'Salerno'. Battle honours in the Army are only officially awarded after a war to be then emblazoned on the regimental colours.

We stayed in Ostend for two days and then moved on to join the Guards Armoured Division at Hougarde some thirty miles from Brussels. Here the Battalion replaced the 1st (Infantry) Battalion Welsh Guards, now short of reinforcements but which already contained 'X' Company from the disbanded 4th Battalion of the Regiment. In conjunction with the armoured squadron to which they had been 'married', the latter were now able to demonstrate to us the techniques of close tank/infantry cooperation. Right Flank were also doubly fortunate in being about to take over from 'X' Company itself.

While we mainly had newcomers within the ranks of the three platoons, nevertheless, as already mentioned, there was still a steady core of experienced NCOs who had been in North Africa or Italy. Company HQ too was a conglomeration of old-stagers, including Chadwick (who had been captured with me and later escaped) driving the company carrier. Benson still poured out his invectives as company runner and Company Sergeant-Major Lindsay was as reliable as ever.

Operation codeword 'Veritable' was about to start and we moved to an assembly area in a large Trappist monastery near Tilburg where German flying bombs roared overhead on their way to Antwerp and we could see the occasional sky-trail of a V2 on its way to London. I felt very sorry for the monks having their vows of silence broken by an infantry battalion, especially as the Germans would now have been justified in bombing it as a military target. There was supposed to be a deserter there from the East Lancashire Regiment, tonsure and all; but I never saw him. He must have found the silence a bit of a strain when the novelty had worn off. An enterprising member of Right Flank had his head shaved in a tonsure too as he said it fitted his steel helmet better. Everyone kept a close watch on him!

A fierce battle was now raging in the Reichswald forest just to the west of the Rhine which was the first portion of German territory to be invaded by the Allies. The rains hampered all troop movements and turned the roads into rivers. Around Goch and Cleves the Germans were now disputing every inch of the way and trying to stem the hammer blows of the British and Canadian forces, comprising the 1st Canadian Army under the command of a Canadian general. The days dragged on with still no scope for an armoured division to deploy or capture the Rhine bridge at Wesel which was our main objective.

There were continuous postponements. We were at first to be reserve infantry battalion of the Guards Armoured Division, to allow us to become properly trained and married into a new tank/infantry battle group. These tank/infantry battle groups had been formed after the initial Normandy landings which had shown the need for such new combinations. The one we were joining (replacing 'X' Company) had spearheaded the Division's 100-mile-dash in one day to capture Brussels. But thereafter they had been held up by the totally unsuitable tank terrain interspersed by canals and elevated roadways. So they had failed to connect in time with the beleaguered British and Polish paratroops which had been landed at Arnhem.

Each battle group of the Guards Armoured Division comprised an infantry and a tank battalion of the same regiment. Thus the Welsh battle group had their own 1st Battalion of infantry and 2nd Battalion of tanks. The men mostly knew each other and the officers shared messes; so an existing regimental sense of identity supported that of the joint battle group.

These new formations were the brainchild of Major-General Allan Adair commanding the Guards Armoured Division and from lessons learned during the Normandy fighting when tanks and infantry at first tended to fight separately. So he formed Grenadier, Coldstream, Welsh and Irish Guards battle groups comprising both tanks and infantry fighting and living together in the same regimental combination. The aim was to get the infantry right up on top of the tanks. The Irish Guards battle group even had two Vandeleur cousins, one commanding the armour and the other the matching infantry battalion. Their *esprit de corps* incidentally encapsulated an all-Irish identity, being recruited from both sides of the Irish border, but always with Catholic as opposed to Protestant padres. But their prevailing loyalty was really to the Regiment – rather than to one half of Ireland or the other.

The Welsh armoured/infantry battle group had already received as much needed reinforcements 'X' Company Scots Guards from our disbanded 4th Battalion. The Welsh Guards infantry, however, were about to be replaced by the 2nd Battalion Scots Guards.

Some thought that 'Jocks' and 'Taffs' would be a bad combination; but initial training together soon showed the makings of a good partnership. My company, Right Flank, were particularly fortunate in having 2 Squadron Welsh Guards with whom to form our partnership; for it was this same squadron which had lately partnered our own 'X' Company. This squadron and Right Flank now formed a squadron/company battle group to train together in tank/infantry fighting. In particular we learnt the technique of the tanks providing a smokescreen through which we could attack enemy positions. Their five troops of three tanks each were usually married to the same infantry platoon. One section of a platoon was also the right number for sitting on top of a single tank. This Welsh Guards battalion exceptionally had Cromwell rather than Sherman tanks, being the best in the Guards Armoured Division. They had greater speed, lower profile and, above all, more flat space for infantry to ride on.

Due to the loss of the Welsh Guards infantry our battle group attempted to be rechristened the 'Celtic Battle Group', to take advantage of some imagined Celtic identity shared between Welsh and Scots. To Glasgow Scots, however, the name 'Celtic' signifies a Catholic as opposed to a Protestant Glasgow football team. So we preferred to call ourselves 'the Scots/Welsh Battle Group' and this name also came to be the official one used in all battle orders.

Our first military engagement was to be entirely detached from the tanks, as we were first sent into action alongside the 51st Highland Division now taking a fearful hammering around Goch and Cleves where every inch of the Reichswald (the only part of the Reich west of the Rhine) was now being resolutely defended. The divisional tanks, including the Battalion, meanwhile remained in reserve at Tilburg.

Awaiting orders to advance, our company officers were now billeted on a rich Dutch coal merchant who was as hospitable as the rest of the Dutch in welcoming 'the Tommies' with open arms. They appeared to have had a terrible time under the Germans; everyone over eighteen had had to live underground or be conscripted to work in Germany. The drummer in his swing band had been shot for selling newspapers and he himself had been beaten up by the Gestapo.

But there were excesses and brutalities too on the Allied side. He told me with great reluctance how two drunken British officers had beaten on his door one night and demanded admittance. He opened it and was ordered at revolver point to find them a woman. He led them down a side street where he managed to struggle free. One fired shots at him in the darkness as he made off, but they were too drunk to shoot straight.

Our orders to move arrived suddenly, as they usually do, in the middle of the night. The darkness became alive with flashing headlights and scurrying feet. We slept fitfully in our TCLs (Troop Carrying Lorries) on the road to Genep. Next morning we marched five miles to take over from the Irish Guards at Hommersom while they put in a daylight attack on what was supposed to be a strongly held sector of the old Siegfried Line – the original defences of the Fatherland – although there appeared to have been no real fortifications to compare with the French Maginot Line.

It was an unwelcome sensation moving through the gunlines as the ground reverberated with the roar of their salvoes fired in support of the 51st Division. But it seemed to be a relatively quiet sector that we eventually took over. In fact the Irish Guards were parading by platoons as we moved in, and being inspected by their officers to see that all was in order before moving off to attack the village of Vrig just in front. Most wore parachutist jackets and stocking caps. Their 'mad' Irish company commander did not apparently believe in steel helmets and boasted that he always led the attack with company HQ in front.

They were about to attack in broad daylight without the supporting tanks of their battle group, apparently because of the soggy nature of the ground. I could see little through my binoculars as trees obstructed my view. At first I only saw the airbursts and smoke screen put down by our artillery. Then there was silence for a few minutes with the distant stutter of small arms fire. Then the area in front suddenly sprouted columns of smoke and reverberated with the sound of bursting shells. Some said it was our own artillery but, quite obviously, it was not; I could hear the familiar sound of German Nebelwerfers screaming through the air. I pitied the poor Micks.

For nothing better to do we began to cook some looted poultry as we were now on German territory – although still to the west of the Rhine. Then, as it began to get dark, word came through that the Irish Guards were being withdrawn from their objective where floods had prevented their survivors from digging in. The enemy defensive fire had taken a heavy toll and eight of their carriers had been blown up on mines. We were told that the Irish Guards company would infiltrate back in the darkness to their former positions. We were to give them preference in our billets and do all we could to make them comfortable. We prepared all the German chickens that we had left and also put on a brew of tea; but there were only about twenty men who came trudging back under one officer in the darkness. They were absolutely dead beat. A few were lightly wounded; but many were too exhausted to continue to their regimental aid post and simply lay down to sleep where they were, soaked to the skin. The ground had been waterlogged and owing to the machine-gun and mortar fire, they had had to lie full length in the water. Their Company Sergeant-Major was terrific, talking in a detached way about the NCOs he had nurtured; how he knew they would always do well. He described how a certain sergeant had killed four Germans before being shot himself; and also how his major (Mad Mick) had charged two machine-guns with rifle and bayonet before another firing from behind a house had riddled him. (He was later posthumously awarded the Victoria Cross.)

Those now billeted with us, however, could not take this massacre of all their friends and talked fitfully into the night of how they had last seen mates with legs blown off crying for the stretcher-bearers who could not get near for the machine-gun fire. I shut them up, saying it was never so bad as it seemed at first; and that half of them would turn up next morning. I then moved my new men out of earshot for it was not good for them to hear this sort of talk when they had never been in action before.

Next morning it transpired that in this daylight attack on Vrig the Irish Guards had lost two company commanders, and many platoon officers and other ranks killed or wounded. We also heard the German wireless boasting of their success.

Just before we moved off to take over other positions on our right the Irish Company Sergeant-Major got his men out of their houses to be formally inspected by their surviving Second-in-Command. They were a sorry sight compared with yesterday's parade as they filed out blinking with fatigue into the morning sunlight. Most of their uniforms were in tatters, few wore headdress, and many wore field dressings. But the Sergeant-Major was intent that everything should be done properly and that a sense of pride be restored to the battered remnants of his unit. 'Company – Get on parade!' They all sprang to attention as one man, sloped arms perfectly and formed up in the middle of the road. The Sergeant-Major turned round and saluted the Second-in-Command. 'There are sixty-six guardsmen missing parade, sir; otherwise Company present and ready for your inspection, sir!'

It was a refreshing contrast now to be living among the guardsmen again after the segregation of an officers' mess. We were no longer in support of the 51st Division, but were back under command of the Guards Armoured Division and married again to our Welsh Guards Tank Battalion as a joint battle group.

The full scope of Allied strategy was now apparent as the long-awaited American offensive to our south started with the crossing of the Roer, after the floods had subsided following the blowing by the Germans of the Roer dams. It was mainly grounded parachutists which the Germans were deploying against the British and Canadian forces in the north. In the Reichswald it had been the toughest fighting since Normandy under adverse conditions of pouring rain and flooded supply routes. The basic strategy had also been similar to that of Normandy with a series of hammer blows by British and

Canadian infantry to attract the German reserves. Then a subsequent right hook by the Americans now leading to their crossing of the Rhine over a bridge they had managed to capture intact at Remagen.

Our division was now given the task of attacking the concentrated German pocket at Kapellan, still on the west side of the Rhine. I obtained billets for my platoon in a bombed house and sent them foraging down what remained of the village street to supplement our evening meal of army rations. We put our findings on a large table. There were seven sides of ham, three honeycombs and enough eggs for a gargantuan omelette. For dessert we had a choice of bottled cherries, loganberries or strawberries from the well-stocked cellars – all this washed down with excellent Rheinwein and sparkling Moselle. It was not a bad life.

After this huge repast I went down to the cellar with Sergeant Stewart to where I had noticed a bricked-up door with the cement still wet. At last the hole was big enough to crawl through and our torches lit up the priceless interior. It revealed the carefully stored contents of a bombed shop; for every town and village had been destroyed by Allied bombers in this area. Four brand new Hohner piano accordions found their way into our hands to enliven an evening party. We already had a platoon band consisting of swing pianist, accordion and guitar. By ten o'clock 'Loch Lomond' was being 'swung'. By eleven o'clock an older member had grown sentimental and was singing 'Lilli Marlene', the old Afrika Korps favourite, later adopted by the 8th Army. At midnight I stopped the party and ordered everyone to bed. Five miles away the night was dangerous, and I knew that we were to put in an attack next morning. What a curious kind of war this was compared with Italy.

At 5 a.m. I was summoned by a shake on the shoulder and the words: 'You're wanted at Company Headquarters for an orders group right away, sir!' We debussed at Kapellan just short of the Rhine at 0730 hrs and by forced march found ourselves on the start-line at 1100 hrs. Our job was to clear a large wooded area known to be occupied by the Germans and leading up to the banks of the Rhine. Right Flank was appropriately on the right with 'G' Company on the left, and the other two companies in reserve.

A roar of guns firing behind us, a whistling of shells overhead, a reverberating crump in front and 2SG were off again. I felt slightly apprehensive as our supporting barrage was bursting much too far in front for my liking. So, as pace-keeper on the right, I moved the whole company forward at the run till the sound of purring shrapnel caused reassurance to the older soldiers like myself but discomfort to the new. One has to keep right up under a barrage for it to be effective.

I began to doubt that we would see any Germans, especially when some fine cock pheasants arose from the bracken at my feet. Suddenly the platoon on my left started firing from the shoulder as they moved. I thought this must be some kind of new battle drill, and I cursed one of my men who, being slightly behind me, put a shot right past my ear. All of a sudden I realised that there were a number of Germans getting up from slit trenches just in front and running away. Everyone now started firing indiscriminately and I yelled at them to stop as they were holding up the advance by standing still with their wild unaimed shooting. All the same I lent against a tree and took careful aim with my Sten gun at a German some sixty yards off who was projecting head and shoulders above his trench without surrendering. I felt rather guilty when he toppled over. We all broke into a run and my German was smiling feebly as I passed. I don't think he was too badly wounded. We took a lot of prisoners from the surrounding dug-outs; but when we emerged from the wood found that our charge had now brought us too near our own shells for comfort. We hugged the ground while the last salvo landed sixty yards away. But this very proximity had confused the Germans. We had the satisfaction of seeing two of those retreating go down in the middle of our shellfire.

When the barrage lifted I attacked a group of farm buildings with my platoon, while covered by Victor de Soissons's platoon on the left. We took sixteen Germans out of it including an officer with a Leica camera. Some tried to escape over a field to the left but Victor's Bren gunner shot four of them.

Meanwhile on our right a German platoon we had apparently bypassed came over to Company HQ when they saw the Welsh Guards tanks coming up. This brought the company's bag of prisoners to over a hundred. They were from the 1062 Grenadier Regiment; but they appeared to have little fight left in them at this stage of the war.

Everyone was now flushed with success. Our final objective could be seen across two open fields. We had to wait, however, till the troops on our right were level in case we should be enfiladed; and then we moved up to our objective. Here the ground was soft sand in contrast to the hard Italian rock, which was fortunate as the German shelling was now up to Italian standards. Among those walking about we had four light casualties from tree bursts. One could dig four feet deep in ten minutes and it was quite safe in a slit trench once it was roofed over. It was also a great advantage knowing instinctively when to take cover from the whine of an approaching shell.

My old platoon sergeant from Italy, Sergeant Macphee, had a steel helmet which was much too small for him. He looked somewhat comic wearing it perched on top of his domed head; in Italy he had preferred to wear an old stocking cap. He came from a croft on South Uist and was the most dependable of characters. He always referred to the enemy as 'the Bosch'.

Victor now sent a section of his platoon forward to some farm houses, but one of them was shot by a sniper. Once the mines had all been removed from the tracks to our rear, the Welsh Guards tanks came up and 'brewed up' these farms one after another. This was usual in case they held snipers. It was also too easy. The tanks simply fired a belt of incendiary bullets into the red-tiled roofs which were lined with straw for warmth. In a minute they were blazing infernos. I could not bear to see the suffering of the animals in this European war. The toll of burnt cattle was appalling as our tanks advanced setting all the farmsteads on fire. The fields too were full of cattle and horses wounded by shrapnel. They seemed so patient and resigned about it all, continuing to graze till, overcome by loss of blood, they lay down and died. As rigor mortis set in the legs of the cattle would point in grotesque angles at the sky.

There was a lot of shelling now as the German artillery was forced into the rapidly diminishing Wesel pocket, which was only some fifteen miles across. 'F' Company got the worst of it in the wood which they had just captured and the Battalion's casualties now mounted to eight killed and twenty-five wounded. Sergeant-Major Lumsden of 'F' Company was shouting 'Get some slit trench service in!' when he was mortally wounded by one of our own shells falling short. It was 6 March 1945 and the second anniversary of the Battle of Medenine when he had won the Military Medal for knocking out two German tanks. He had won the DCM at Salerno for rescuing his platoon officer caught on barbed wire at the tobacco factory. He had won a bar to his MM on Monte Camino.

Next morning we moved off to take up new positions for the next advance. Left Flank moved down to the River Roer, which they managed to cross under heavy fire over a mined bridge which was then blown up behind them. Nevertheless it was soon repaired.

My platoon was now in reserve on top of a ridge. One of our artillery observation officers was sent up as it offered a perfect view over the German-held valley beyond – although I hardly expected him to approach across the open in a Sherman tank, especially when the Germans started shelling us in consequence. He parked the tank behind the house. However, he most effectively demolished a church steeple from which it was suspected the Germans were directing artillery fire on our positions.

My company was to lead the attack next day at 4 p.m. This was to be our first full infantry/tank battle group attack and it was reassuring to see all our Cromwells roaring up into position on the ridge from where they started shooting up all the houses on the plain below. We were now attacking from a salient with our flanks unprotected. Some German self-propelled guns proceeded to shoot at our tanks just as we were threading our way through them. It was a novel experience wondering which side of a tank to dodge behind when the shells came down.

My platoon now entered a deep gulley leading down to a bridge. Suddenly there was an explosion on the bank just above as a shell landed. Then a blinding roar as another came right into the gulley itself. I felt a bit shaken, but there was simply no shelter to be had nor way of getting out of the deep-sided gulley. A signaller was wounded beside me. Then I heard the whine of yet another approaching shell which I instinctively felt was coming straight for me. But being in the gulley there was nothing I could do. There was a blinding flash and I found myself staring blankly at a small, smoking crater straight in front of my feet. Although my body must have hit the ground, I found myself in the curious position of thinking that I was looking down on myself. My reactions were, 'My God, I must be absolutely riddled', as I noticed, in a detached way, blood beginning to flow down my left side. Dazed, I staggered to a company carrier where I must have collapsed having lost a great deal of blood on the way. My trousers and jacket were soaked; but I felt no pain, only a general numbness and faintness.

The carrier rushed me back to the Regimental Aid Post where dressings were applied and I drank cups of hot sweet tea which soon much revived me. It was now evident that there was more blood than damage from a number of subsidiary wounds. One piece of shrapnel had lodged in my left arm, another had gone clean through my hand without breaking a bone. The only pain I felt was from a number of surface lacerations which caused great discomfort when I tried to swallow. I was lucky. The shell had burst right at my feet and my compass, which I then wore on my belt, had embedded in it a large piece of shrapnel which would otherwise have gone straight into my middle.

As part of an ambulance-load of wounded we bumped back to a casualty clearing station. Some were in exhilarated mood at being out of harm's way – but one guardsman was ashen-grey and very silent. That night quite a collection of our nineteen-year-old subalterns were brought in, one hit in the elbow, then John Swinton with a bullet in his leg. There was a roar of applause with each new arrival. Lastly came Neil Torrance who for some reason was running about as pleased as Punch with a bullet in his chest.

I learnt later that Graham Gow had been killed by a shell in Right Flank shortly after I was wounded. He always thought he was going to die. The battle group had run into trouble with German parachutists down by the railway-line, where the few tanks which had managed to cross the river before the bridge collapsed were knocked out by an SP gun. The attack, nevertheless, appeared to have been a success. All our main objectives had been taken before nightfall with 110 prisoners from 22 and 24 Parachutist Regiments of the 1st Parachutist Army. Unfortunately the shelling had become severe next morning which raised the Battalion's casualties to eight killed and thirty-three wounded.

This was the last attack before the Germans withdrew from the south bank and blew the Rhine bridge at Wesel. It was also the end of Operation Veritable.

I, of course, knew none of this until later and did not even remember much about my journey back from the front except that, at every medical clearing station, the doctors seemed dissatisfied with my medical ticket and undid all my bandages to examine and probe my wounds – which I much disliked. I also had twice-hourly injections of penicillin. While I was out for the count someone made off with my pair of Veltdschoen boots and, worse still, my small pack which contained a month's advance of pay which I had just drawn for a projected trip to Brussels.

The same afternoon I was flown in an RAF Dakota to Brussels. Next day I was operated on in 108 General Hospital to have the shrapnel removed. What a complete contrast to the war in Italy. Three days later I had another operation. Penicillin soon sorted me out and I was on my feet again in a few days, left only with small pieces of harmless shrapnel still in my neck and shoulders.

After three weeks I was walking about in uniform in Brussels with my arm in a sling. The Belgians were enthusiastically friendly, conceding their seats to me in tramcars. For days after my stitches had been removed I guiltily wore my arm in a sling, although this was by then quite unnecessary! A further three weeks and I was almost well again. The sun was shining and I could rarely remember such a beautiful spring. I felt brimming again with health and consumed vast meals in the Epaule de Mouton near the Grande Place. Brussels looked lovely with all the street-barrows full of flowers.

One afternoon I travelled by bus to the Field of Waterloo. It was a glorious spring day with the chestnut trees bursting into green, and apple blossom in all the orchards. A valley of sprouting corn was the site of the famous battle in June 1815 lasting one day and involving the deployment of 100,000 men – but with the British and Germans against the French. Wellington on occasions must have been able to glimpse his opponent Napoleon on the opposite ridge. Here 25,000 Europeans had been killed in one day, along with 5,000 horses. But now all was peaceful and serene. The farmers were ploughing and larks sang in a blue sky. I walked down to the still-surviving farmhouse of Hougoumont, rebuilt where it had been damaged. Hens were dusting themselves by a small chapel in the courtyard where so many wounded had died. I walked into the orchard where a huge wall still contained the loopholes made by the defending Scots Guardsmen who had held back the massed infantry attacks of Reille's corps. In one corner there was even a tablet bearing the regimental badge.

Most out-of-bed patients of the Brussels hospital were now being posted home on convalescent leave. Some instinct, however, told me I must refuse home leave although most other officers in the hospital were taking it. Home could only be the Battalion while the war was still on. Nevertheless I felt something of a fool when I emerged triumphant from the Colonel's office after he had been trying to persuade me to take home leave now that the war was almost over. Two other officers of the Battalion who had just been wounded also did the same – for the 'pull' of the Battalion was too great. This however required the technicality of being signed on as fit.

Frank Waldron now promised me a lift back to the Battalion rear

HQ next morning, which had the great advantage of avoiding the tedium and delay of the more regular channels of transport. Hitch-hiking indeed was an accepted method, although two officers were arrested by the Provost Marshal of Brussels for 'deserting' back to the Battalion as being technically 'absent while on sick leave'.

9

Advance into Germany

Driving among the supply convoys on 2 April 1945, Frank Waldron took me right across the Maas to Genep where we joined a reinforcement company and then drove across the Rhine on a new pontoon bridge. We then moved into farm buildings near Bocholt. Stray German prisoners brought in from nearby woods caused great excitement among all the new officers waiting there to join various battalions for the first time.

The Corps Commander, General Horrocks, had now launched 30 Corps including the Guards Armoured Division on its long delayed advance right into Germany. The codeword for this operation was, appropriately enough, 'Plunder'. To the south, other Allied divisions were also advancing east of the Rhine against scattered German resistance. But to the north the German Corps Ems, containing the 6th, 7th and 8th Parachutist Divisions (all grounded since Crete) and the 15th Panzer Division, still confronted 30 Corps and the 1st Canadian Army. These German units now proceeded to do all they could to impede our invasion of their Fatherland.

The Guards Armoured Division got off to a good start by driving north-east up the old Dutch-German border with 2SG riding on the backs of the Welsh Guards' tanks. Everywhere they were mobbed by cheering Dutch. One of our officers, who had married a Dutch girl, even managed to liberate his Dutch mother-in-law. Then the centre line of advance continued for twenty miles to Nordhorn, just over the German border.

I set out for Enschede in the back of a 3-ton lorry to catch up with the Battalion's supply point. There were twenty of us in the lorry without a weapon between us, which I thought unwise considering all the stray Germans who had been surrendering in this area during the day. Next morning I cadged a further lift by truck to the Battalion near Lingen. We passed through Nordhorn where the bridge had collapsed after being partly blown in face of the advance, but had now been speedily rebuilt by our engineers. Everywhere was the bustle and expectation of an armoured division in full advance. There was a constant forward flow of heavy vehicles and backward rush of jeeps and scout cars on their way to Divisional Headquarters.

The Scots/Welsh battle group headquarters was now in a village just short of Lingen and everyone there was full of the previous night's exploits. There had been a unique night attack by tanks and infantry. As we approached Lingen we could see the road was lined with charred bodies (like burnt wood) at the side of gutted vehicles. Horses and timbers were scattered in confusion on both sides of the road. There were some knocked out 88 mms on trailers. I thought this must all have been the work of rocket-firing aircraft, till I saw the fresh blood of the horses and noticed that some of the trucks were still smouldering indicating that this was in fact the work of the previous night. With all these dead horses it looked like the field of Waterloo.

Apparently Corps Headquarters had gained intelligence that the 7th Parachutist Division were building up a new defensive line on the Dortmund–Ems canal eighteen miles in front. The plan was simple. It was for the Scots/Welsh battle group to advance through the night with the infantry riding on the leading tanks, and capture intact the double bridge at Lingen over the canal before it could be blown. Tanks do not usually advance in the dark.

They set out from Nordhorn with Right Flank riding on 2 Squadron's tanks and Left Flank on 3 Squadron following. The bridge there was only half-blown but, after they had crossed, it collapsed, cutting them off from the following company/squadrons. My company on top of 2 Squadron's tanks nevertheless continued the advance in unorthodox fashion at top speed through the darkness, with headlights full on. There was some sporadic enemy fire but nothing much, for the tanks were travelling at high speed and took the Germans with all their horsedrawn transport completely by surprise.

Guardsman Chadwick told me he had been left behind at one point and when speeding to catch up in his carrier he suddenly found himself round a corner looking straight down the barrel of an 88 mm. All brakes were crashed on, the carrier swivelled round and into the nearest field; but it turned out to be one of two which had just been knocked out on their towing chassis.

The Welsh squadron had then run into a whole convoy of horses and MT transport withdrawing over the Dortmund–Ems Canal.

They must have got the shock of their lives. Our guardsmen on top of the tanks shot the German riders and the tanks with full headlights on, charged down the horses, firing in all directions, and knocking the timbers headlong into the ditch. A German motor-cyclist tried to pass and threw a stick grenade on to one of the infantry-laden tanks. Guardsman Bruce sent him flying with a shot from his rifle.

The company dismounted just short of the Ems bridge for a planned assault as dawn was breaking. Another German motor-cyclist came driving up and seemed quite flabbergasted at being stopped; he tried to turn back and was also shot.

9 Platoon then got two sections across the Ems river bridge and the leading tanks were just about to follow and resume the advance when the Germans, suddenly realising what was up, blew the bridge in their faces, showering everybody with masonry. Some 88 mms and flak guns placed in position opened up on the stranded two sections who had to retire over the debris.

So ended a unique tank and infantry night attack. Right Flank were positively cock-a-hoop.

There was considerable shelling next day and Right Flank were withdrawn in the evening to the rear of Battalion Headquarters, where I rejoined them and was given command of no. 7 Platoon again. They had suffered eight casualties the previous night; but were nevertheless obviously very pleased with themselves. Everyone seemed glad to see me again and I even more so to see them.

Ex-Sergeant Wilson, alias 'Joe Plush', was now back, temporarily wearing a top hat instead of a steel helmet. He had been in some kind of army home for war neuroses and in his pack was his tunic ready with the sergeant's stripes on. He was a born comic.

That same afternoon our Household Cavalry armoured cars discovered a bridge that was still intact a few miles upstream, but guarded by German parachutists and some 88 mm guns. A squadron/company battle group of the Coldstream moved into position under cover of an embankment. The squadron commander had thought up the ingenious device of having two aircraft Typhoon rockets attached to either side of his tank turret, to be fired electrically from inside. The first the Germans knew was a series of rockets landing on their position which completely dazed them for a few minutes. Smoke was put down by the tanks followed by an artillery barrage. A Coldstream company commander won the Victoria Cross for running across the long metal bridge and cutting the wires leading to the charges. His company then followed suit and captured the German commander who was frantically pressing the demolition plunger. Further down the road, however, the bridge over the canal itself was blown.

That was the end of this rapid advance. It next took the 53rd Infantry Division two days to clear the parachutists from the town of Lingen, after an assault crossing of the canal itself. It also took the Royal Engineers more time to construct a new bridge as they were by now short of bridging material, having had more repair jobs than it was possible for them to contend with. Indeed they were to have to construct over fifty new bridges before reaching the German coast and its naval base at Cuxhaven from which Admiral Doenitz was conducting the main German defence. Hitler and Goebbels had now retired into their Berlin bunker.

Two days' respite unfortunately now gave Corps Ems time to reorganise their Panzerjäger armed with portable anti-tank Panzerfausts, which had just come into use and were ideal anti-tank weapons in close country. At that time we had no such anti-tank weapons apart from Piats, which had no effect whatsoever on a large tank or self-propelled gun.

30 Corps now had to fight every inch of the way into northern Germany. Indeed the German 6th and 7th Parachute Divisions never lost control of the situation until the very end when the cease-fire had sounded. It was infantry fighting all the way with just enough mobility to warrant the use of tanks; but the Division paid the toll in their halting progress of some eighty knocked out. While the Allies had complete control of the air this did not make much difference in such close country.

On 5 April, however, the Luftwaffe flattered us with one of their last appearances. They came in at roof-top level but beyond wounding some gunners and putting a bullet through the roof of Support Company's officers' mess, they did little damage. Next morning we lined up to continue the advance, with the Scots/Welsh battle group now leading. Our objective was Furstenau where the 53rd Division had reported Germans just down the road. 'Joe Plush' was re-promoted just before we moved off. His lance-sergeant's tunic was immediately taken out of his pack and donned by the roadside as our troop-carrying lorries (TCLs) swung past him. He got a cheer from each in turn as he stood there with hands clasped above his head, giving the boxer's acknowledgement.

'F' Company were now in the lead and bumped into the enemy just outside Lingen where they had prepared new positions. We could hear the moan of the Nebelwerfers coming down on them. It sounded ominous. We sat in the main street for two hours listening to the distant sound of sporadic firing. The street contained the shopping centre where all the windows were smashed open and it was a looter's paradise appropriate to Operation Plunder. There was not very much one could do beyond restricting loot to small articles. The tanks came off best as they could carry everything from typewriters to wireless sets.

At lunchtime we were off again with 'G' Company now leading, having switched north on to 'Spade' route, leaving 'F' Company to extricate themselves. Their company commander, a great personality and leader, was among those killed by SP guns which covered the German minefields. As the Brigade Commander would not countenance the delay of a set piece infantry attack, all battle groups were now despatched on different centre lines to probe for a chink in the enemy's defences. But these narrow roads through woods and villages appeared to be covered on a pre-arranged enemy plan. There was no bridge which the German engineers failed to blow up and every village was protected by log roadblocks. The latter were often defended by parties of Panzerjägers from the 6th and 7th Parachute Divisions.

Our usual formation during the advance was for armoured cars of the Household Cavalry to take the lead when available. They were extremely fast and adept at finding undefended roads for the Division to take as their new centre line. Unlike other vehicles, these armoured cars, when fired upon, could back out of trouble at full speed or turn round in a tight circle. After them came a troop of three tanks which were followed by the remaining tanks of the squadron all carrying infantry on top, whose job it was to jump off and rush straight into the attack. The infantry, however, did not generally sit on the very front tank as they would have been machine-gunned off each time opposition was encountered. It was also only the two leading infantry companies which rode on top of their tanks. The remainder travelled in the TCLs until required for a proper attack. Then the code word 'Magnum' (men on tanks) was given and everyone mounted his particular tank in a pre-arranged place. We had already practised these tank/infantry tactics until they became second nature.

The chief weakness of the German defence strategy in this northern part of Germany was that it was designed on the supposition that their Volksturm or Home Guard would sabotage our supply lines and that the local people would give the Wehrmacht every assistance. In fact the Volksturm, in so far as it existed at all, never fired a shot. The farm people too were quite ready to point out German minefields for us to clear so they could get on with the proper job of tending their animals and mending their homesteads. Most agricultural labour on the farms through which we were now passing appeared to be done by foreign prisoners on parole living in the German farmhouses. Mostly these were Russians, still wearing Russian uniforms, who persisted in saluting me as an officer when they popped up from behind hedges. But surprisingly some were also French prisoners wearing French uniforms. There were no British or Americans.

The other unexpected feature was the number of horses everywhere. Germany appeared to be still the land of the horse and most transport, even in the German army, was still horse-drawn – as was fully apparent when our battle group routed the German horse-drawn convoy at Lingen.

Tony Mannock's platoon was now in the lead but they had not proceeded far before the leading armoured car was fired on by an 88 mm. As the leading tank could not turn the corner to fire at it, Tony went after it with a Piat anti-tank projector. A troop of our tanks then worked round to a flank and knocked out all three 88 mms without a single casualty. The only casualty to the company was Tony himself who got a bullet in his wrist.

We set off again in the late afternoon, past the smouldering German SP guns and out into the countryside beyond. Right Flank was now in the lead, sitting on our tanks as we raced along the roads machine-gunning every hedge, and expecting Germans to emerge at any moment. But darkness soon came upon us. We formed a compact leaguer for the night, in North African desert fashion, around a group of farm houses some two miles in front of the rest of the Battalion.

Suddenly all our TCVs and 15-ton trucks appeared out of the night with their sidelights on, led by a motor-cycle shining its headlights. They were sworn at and told to 'switch off your bloody lights'. Otherwise the darkness remained undisturbed.

It was an unexpected luxury to get blankets, greatcoats and small packs for the night. This was to become the rule rather than the exception. It was certainly good for morale to be able to keep warm and well fed, even in a slit trench; and so very different from Italy.

Next morning at seven o'clock we were off again with my platoon and our Welsh Guards tanks now in the lead. Just as we were about to start, a concentrated barrage of airbursts exploded directly overhead and we jumped off the tanks to shelter beneath. One man was wounded. This turned out to be an opening barrage from our own long-range medium artillery, shooting in support from map references – just to let the Germans know we were coming. The artillery officer travelling with us in his tank finally managed to get his guns stopped after which we set off again down the road at 30 m.p.h. in the freezing sunshine.

We advanced about six miles without seeing any Germans, although we kept our fingers on our triggers all the way. Just outside Langerich the leading troop commander wirelessed back that there was a roadblock just in front and that he had seen some German infantry around it.

I jumped off my tank and ran along the road with my platoon and then ordered Sergeant ('Joe Plush') Wilson with his section to fire at the enemy from the front while I advanced with another section to attack the German position from the left flank. Sergeant Wilson, always the comic, was shouting 'Splendid! Come on my men, charge!' and disappeared amid a roar of laughter in the direction of the roadblock. I came out to the side and except for a couple of Germans running away, at whom I fired and missed, there was nothing to be seen. Sergeant Wilson's section were now getting to work dismantling the roadblock of tree trunks to let our tanks through.

Suddenly from behind there was a roar of approaching shells and we dived for the nearest ditches. The shells were right on top of us and the ground shook. There were shouts for help and the stench of cordite. Two or three lay wounded. It was clearly our own medium guns again firing from behind and 'Joe Plush' lay in the middle of the road in a pool of blood. We picked him up but his eyes already had the glassy stare of the dead.

Another salvo of shells from our medium artillery descended as I found myself hugging the earth in a mixture of fury and terror. I had never even asked for this 'help'. There was a shout again for stretcher-bearers as the smoke cleared. I felt a blind ungovernable fury and ran down the road to where the artillery observation officer was sitting in his scout car, the turret of which was closed against his own flying shrapnel. In my anger I jumped on the top and battered on the turret with my Sten gun. It was gingerly opened and a head emerged. I swore at him to stop his damned mediums wiping out my platoon. He said they must be German guns and I told him if he would get out of his tank turret he would soon learn to distinguish between German shells and our own. Eventually he said he would stop them; but something was wrong with his wireless for it took him quite a time.

Having stopped our artillery 'support' fire, we now got to work on demolishing the German roadblock to let our tanks through. I grouped my three sections in ditches among the trees on either side of the road. Preoccupied with the work of clearance, I suddenly became aware that at the top of the hill 200 yards away straight in front, the Germans had a large heavily camouflaged gun pointing straight down the road at us. They had timed things to a nicety. I must have been in its sights several times as I crossed and re-crossed the road. When the pioneer officer and some of his men were pushing aside a huge log, the enemy gun suddenly opened fire. They hit the pioneer officer and blew the leg off another man. A guardsman beside me also had his arm blown off. Clearly with my casualties and the lack of cover we could not assault the gun frontally up the road. The only course was for us to provide covering fire while another platoon attacked from the right. The gun itself, which I could now see quite clearly, was situated near the top of the hill through which the road ran in a gulley.

I ran back to Digby Raeburn, my company commander, who instructed Victor's platoon to mount the assault from the right. We then put down smoke with our 2-inch mortar and a lot of Bren gun fire while they edged round the right flank. A troop of our tanks, seeing the trouble we were in, also worked round into a supporting position on the left where unfortunately all three were promptly knocked out, one after the other, by a German self-propelled gun enfilading them from behind. A machine-gun also opened up on Victor's assaulting platoon causing them to drop flat as some fell wounded. Sergeant White's leading section, which I could now see quite clearly, nevertheless continued attacking while we fired magazine after magazine into the German positions surrounding the gun. Sergeant White out in front ran so close to our fire that I thought we might have hit him; for he could be seen going bald-headed for the gun itself. He shot down most of its crew with his automatic before being shot dead himself. Eight Germans were found dead around the gun when we reached it.

Sergeants White and Wilson were two of the last NCOs left in the company from Italy. Sergeant White was put in for a posthumous Victoria Cross but to no avail. Such awards tend only to follow what are regarded as outstanding operations from the viewpoint of Higher Command.

To cap it all, the medium artillery now lifted 200 yards on to our new positions and caused three more casualties to Victor's platoon – as if we had not had enough already. Our three burning tanks on the ridge to our left belched flame and smoke and crackled and roared like furious monsters, as all their ammunition and shells exploded. No one, fortunately, had been left inside.

I set one of our German prisoners to dig a slit trench for me. He was under eighteen and said he had never been in action before. Then I went and sat by myself on a bank. I was soaked to the skin with the sweat of exertion and felt completely exhausted.

Two companies now passed through us to take Lengerich where the Typhoons had been strafing. I hardly noticed them. That night I lay in my slit trench gazing up at the starlit heavens. It was quite comfortable and warm for I now had sheets, a pillow and a mattress from a nearby farmhouse. I slept like a log and next day felt quite revived again. It was a beautiful morning as we sat among our vehicles in the sunshine; but somehow it seemed strangely quiet without 'Joe Plush''s banter and 'horror' stories. He had certainly contributed much to company morale over the years. It was not exactly that he had been a good soldier, although at times, apparently with tongue in cheek, he had acted the part to perfection. It was his irrepressible good humour. The more the 'horrors' occurred, the more he laughed and everyone with him.

We were glad to leave this area of burnt-out farmhouses. What we had at first taken to be a row of charred beams in a gutted cowshed, turned out, through the attraction of myriads of flies, to be cattle burnt alive at their halters. I could not understand why the Germans did not let them loose when they saw all the farmhouses being turned into funeral pyres in the wake of our advancing tanks. For fear of snipers every single farm house within range of the road was set alight by our tanks' incendiary bullets. In a matter of minutes they were all ablaze with the tethered animals still inside, including many horses.

As the sun went down and the time for leaguering approached, the shooting stopped. There was no point in burning one's prospective billets for the night; even if they might harbour a sniper or two.

Next day the Seconds-in-Command of the Battalion and of the Welsh Guards tank battalion were travelling together in a scout car when they took a wrong turning and were hit by a Panzerfaust. This killed one and badly wounded the other. Digby Raeburn therefore had to leave Right Flank to act as Second-in-Command of the Battalion, which was a great loss.

Left Flank were now in the lead with 4 Tank Squadron on a new centre line along a number of subsidiary roads crossing several small canals. The Germans as usual had all the bridges prepared for demolition – this time with aircraft bombs. 'G' Company managed to capture one of the bridges intact, but lost a new platoon officer who had only arrived that day. We passed through them and were once again leading platoon. As usual we advanced with the tanks machine-gunning every hedge and farmhouse. I was not so sure of the wisdom of these tactics when all the bridges were prepared for demolition. The Germans could hear us a mile off, and could also see the columns of smoke rising from the burning farmhouses. Then bang would go the bridge! During these three weeks our divisional engineers had to rebuild or repair twenty-four of them. However, our tanks could take no chances among the hedgerows with all the Panzerfaust parties around.

It nevertheless gave one a savage thrill riding through enemy territory on the back of our tanks as their guns sprayed tracer from side to side. Whenever we saw anything suspicious the infantrymen sitting on top of the tanks would also open up with their Bren guns. I remember seeing a figure in green uniform running along a hedge. He may have been a German soldier, but could have been a Russian worker, as he was by himself. Someone fired a Bren gun at him and then the whole tankload of infantry followed suit. He was completely riddled.

The tanks were machine-gunning one farmhouse we passed when an old bearded figure rushed to the door waving a large white sheet. The tanks could not stop firing in time and he gradually collapsed in the doorway – symbolic of the utter savagery of war.

Sometimes when we stopped for the night, four men of our Welsh Guards tank troop would form a small choir and sing beautifully in Welsh, ending with 'Land of my Fathers'.

The Germans blew the next bridge when we came to it and Sergeant Macphee, my old platoon sergeant from Italy, now in temporary command of 8 Platoon, got ladders to cross it and hold the far bank so that our indefatigable engineers could repair it.

My platoon were now grouped round some burning farm buildings. The terrified farmer and his wife and daughters were clustered in a trench in the garden with their three Polish farm workers. When one half of the building collapsed in a shower of sparks, I suddenly realised that there were a lot of animals inside about to be burnt to death. We opened the pens to release some young calves which came rushing out. Also surrounded by fire were two beautiful horses of cavalry type. They just stood there giving an occasional whinny, too terrified to gallop through the flames. I told the German farmer to get them out, and he seemed amazed at this concession. Later I allowed him one small room which was not burnt out; but kept the other as my HQ. In return his wife brought me wine and dozens of eggs for the platoon from her store. We piled them into buckets of water and put them to cook on part of a burning outhouse.

During the night 'F' Company reported a number of Germans moving up in front where Dick Berridge had just been killed on patrol. A German quartermaster-sergeant with his ration cart had driven into our lines not realising that we were so near or that a new bridge was being built. All three prisoners wore brand new uniforms, which looked slightly ominous. As I was to be leading platoon next day I made what I hoped was a fighting speech to my men saying that this was now our chance to get to grips with the enemy and revenge ourselves for all the recent casualties we had suffered. In the absence of sergeants I now had only corporals as section commanders (including two Stewart cousins). They were all keen and soon had their men cleaning and oiling their weapons for the morrow. All working parts were soon clicking to our satisfaction. We then slept fitfully through the night by the light of the smouldering farm house.

Next morning there was a sharp frost and thick fog reduced visibility to only twenty yards. I had my platoon ready for zero hour at 8.30 a.m.; but the start had to be postponed owing to the dense fog which was a danger to tanks advancing through it. I hated this waiting and walked up and down outside Company HQ, chain-smoking cigarettes and feeling a heavy responsibility for all the lives in my hands. But my guardsmen were in excellent mood and I could hear them laughing through the pall of mist.

At last came the order to advance through the now thinning fog. We climbed on top of our tanks and rattled across the next bridge where 'F' Company held the far bank; then past their leading sections into the white haze beyond. We had only gone a few hundred yards when our leading tank wirelessed back for my platoon to come up at once. At the same moment we realised that we had driven in the mist right into the middle of some German positions. We jumped off the tanks shooting at a range so point-blank that the Germans had no time for reaction. We then formed into line and rushed through their positions in a small wood. One German was lying on top of a bank clasping a Panzerfaust. I did not know whether he was feigning death or about to fire at the nearest tank so I shot him and he rolled down the bank. I took deliberate aim at another with my Sten gun, and put two shots straight through his chest. He rose up smiling sickly with his hands above his head and tottered off down the road. The stretcher-bearers told me afterwards he had managed to get a hundred yards before being put on a stretcher. The remainder of the Germans then surrendered.

We continued up the road in file just in front of the tanks − it is unfair to expect tanks to take the lead in such close country. We came to some more German positions, some of whose occupants surrendered. But others in a slit trench to our left started throwing hand grenades. These did no damage although one landed within a few yards of myself and Corporal Stewart. We tried to shoot back but could not get a clear shot over the bank. When I tried to fire from the top of a tank a bullet hit its turret so I got down hurriedly. I then sent four men in behind one of Hugh Griffiths's tanks and they extricated the Germans without further trouble.

Further up the road were three trenches on top of a bank in which the German occupants were again keeping down. Corporal Stewart rushed up to them and, lifting his Schmeisser above his head, put a burst into each, killing the occupants. He was taking no chances. Captured German Schmeissers were clearly much better than Lee-Enfield rifles for this kind of fighting; and indeed the German infantry were better armed than ourelves with our old Lee-Enfield rifles and useless Piats.

The mist was now lifting slightly as the sun came up. Astride the road about a hundred yards ahead one could see the last of the German platoon positions. The newly-turned earth from their slit trenches showed up, with their coal scuttle helmets appearing over the top; but in between there was an open field with no cover. With my tank troop commander we decided on a frontal attack while we still had the momentum. My friend Hugh Griffiths, who commanded the leading troop, appreciated the situation, which we had practised before, and was willing for his tanks to go in front until just outside Panzerfaust range. Then he would halt, putting down smoke while we charged through the smokescreen.

It worked perfectly, just as we had so often practised. A section advanced in a huddle behind each of the three tanks while the bullets intended for us rattled off their fronts and the tanks belted Besa at the enemy. One man was killed next to me as we fanned out to attack; but he was our only casualty. He had only joined us the night before. We killed one German and a tank blew another to pieces, as he tried to run away. The remainder surrendered.

We were congratulated over the wireless and ordered to consolidate while Victor's platoon took up the advance. My platoon felt as pleased as Punch for having defeated a whole company of parachutists, taken about fifty prisoners, killed about eight and wounded many more. We had indeed avenged ourselves for the previous day. Victor came up with his platoon and asked me what the going was like. I said it was easy, and described how we had just managed to take the last German position; but I knew it was not so easy now that the fog had lifted to reveal a sparkling morning.

Almost at once a German sniper hit Hugh Griffiths in the arm as he was protruding from the top of his tank. His absence would be a great loss as he understood all the techniques of close infantry/tank co-operation which might not now be so easy with someone else.

Ten minutes later the stretcher-bearers brought back what remained of poor Victor, covered with a gas-cape. A Panzerfaust had hit the tank he was standing beside talking to its commander; and several of his platoon had also been wounded by Spandau fire.

A general attack was now ordered on Menslage for the afternoon. The artillery killed a lot of Germans who were not yet properly dug in and about 150 prisoners were taken. A German success of the afternoon, however, was when an 88 mm battery managed to knock out two or three of our tanks and a half-track.

German prisoners now came running back down the road, their hands above their heads, their greatcoats flapping, shouting, 'Don't shoot, don't shoot!' in German. When they slowed down from exhaustion someone fired a burst at their feet to make them double, then off they set again amidst a roar of laughter. But somehow I could not feel party to such maltreatment: this was far from how the 16th Panzer Division had treated me at Salerno. It was also noticeable that new troops were more savage in this respect than the veterans; I always found that the older sergeants from desert days had a sneaking regard for 'Jerry' as a soldier. New troops had a more civilian and brutal outlook.

That night we became temporarily non-operational as the Coldstream tank/infantry battle group cleared up the remainder of the German parachutists in the woods beyond. So it was now possible for the tank and infantry officers of our joint battle group to sit down to a sumptuous dinner in the dining room of a large farmhouse where we were now billeted. The champagne, of which we now had stacks, flowed freely and brilliant candelabra lit the large table.

We wondered meanwhile what had happened to our civilian Belgian interpreter who had been liberated by the Welsh Guards in Brussels and was always out hunting imaginary SS men. He had been in the Belgian underground movement and thus had an understandable loathing for the Gestapo, intensified rather than modified by his civilian outlook. Two days before, his brother, who was also an interpreter, had been killed along with our Second-in-Command when their scout car was hit by a Panzerfaust. When some German prisoners were brought in for interrogation, he had to be hauled off one man whom he was assaulting in fury.

Now half way through our dinner, when everyone was dining well, the door suddenly burst open and in came our Belgian interpreter dragging an unfortunate German whose face was covered with blood. He knocked him to the ground, lifted him up and knocked him to the ground again, shouting 'There's your SS man!' He was quivering with emotion and dead white. Next exhibits were what he termed 'two SS women'. These looked dignified as they stood with their arms above their heads against the wall and showed no trace of fear before this audience of well-fed, slightly drunk, officers. The man was said by our interpreter to have been a bully and head of the local Nazi Party and the women to have maltreated a Polish child. The Squadron Commander telephoned for permission to shoot the SS man which I hope he did not really mean. But this request was of course refused.

Next morning we set about burying our eight German corpses of the day before. It was just a question of shovelling earth on top of them where they lay in their slit trenches and sticking a rifle in the ground to mark the spot with each victim's steel helmet on top.

IO

The Last Battle

We were now withdrawn for three days for a much-needed rest. Although the fighting conditions were good compared with those in Italy, there had been repeated attacks and we had lost a lot of men. There was also no longer a need for the Guards Armoured Division in XXX Corps as the German 1st Parachutist Army was now narrowly confined within the coastal area between Emden and Bremen. The plan was therefore that other infantry divisions should now hold the enemy compressed into the northern peninsula, and prepare for the final assault on Bremen – the last German stronghold apart from Berlin. The Guards Armoured Division was to move some hundred miles eastwards to join XII Corps and advance on Bremen from the other side – so cutting the Hamburg–Bremen autobahn and threatening the German lines of communication with Berlin. Hitler was now marooned in his Berlin bunker, and the Third Reich was commanded by Admiral Doenitz from the North Sea port of Cuxhaven.

We thus could rest for three days in spring weather, in a countryside undamaged with the fields aflame with yellow cowslips and the beech woods tinged with green. I had not realised that Germany was so preponderantly agricultural and so traditional in its country ways despite much modernisation. Here were oxen as well as horses still pulling the ploughs: unlike in Britain, most transport was then still horse-drawn. Apart from the now flattened industrial Ruhr, Germany appeared to be composed of small farms and picturesque hamlets from which all the men had been conscripted into the armed forces – leaving only the womenfolk to run the farms with the help of a mass of war prisoners on parole. All Germans still appeared to believe in the Fatherland. There was no evidence, as yet, of any collapse of morale, such as had occurred in France after the German breakthrough in the Ardennes.

I entered one farmhouse where the Soviet 'slave' workers were paraded for my benefit by the farmer who told me how much better off they were here than in their own country. These Russians were certainly cheerful enough and as well looked after as our own Italian prisoners-of-war doing similar agricultural work. But in answer to my query all said they wished to get back home. This annoyed the aged German farmer, who snapped at them to take their hands out of their pockets when speaking to an officer! I asked what happened to recalcitrant foreign workers. He said they were few as they preferred to work on German farms rather than be in prison camps; but any offenders were removed by the police to 'correction centres'. He did not, however, wish to elaborate. His farm had to be run somehow with all the younger men now away at the war.

In every village through which we passed, hundreds of such foreign workers became liberated from the nearby farms and 'rural factories' which had been spread throughout the countryside. The French prisoners from four years ago were overjoyed to see us and lined the roads cheering, many now with German girlfriends. They quickly organised themselves into camps awaiting transportation back to France. Some Soviet prisoners, however, were not so spontaneous towards their liberators, if this involved being returned to the Soviet Union. They were of different nationalities, unsure of their identities and whether they really wished to be sent back. These were subsequently to form the 'displaced persons' problem of Europe.

On 17 April 1945 we moved through captured territory to Walsrode. The Battalion set off at dawn on 18 April at the head of 32nd Guards Brigade riding on top of our Welsh Guards' tanks again, with 'F' Company this time in the lead. We were stopped after five miles by unexpectedly heavy opposition outside Kettenburg. Everyone grew impatient. Even my platoon stopped singing and stamping in unison in their TCLs. Whenever we listened over the wireless it was always some code number telling somebody else to 'bash on'. Colonel Henry and the Brigadier came past in their joint scout car. Left Flank was now sent off to find a way through to Ottingen; but also ran into heavy opposition. Some enemy with Panzerfausts even tried to infiltrate back and attack the Welsh Guards' tanks. John Swinton who had returned from hospital the day before, having refused convalescent leave, was badly wounded in the leg which he lost, just as his father had done in the concluding days of the 1914–18 war.

I was now summoned to an orders group. Right Flank and 'G' Company were to take the village of Kettenburg where units of the German 2nd Marine Division were reported to be entrenched. This time I was reserve platoon and there were two new officers in the company to make up for casualties. In this type of warfare such new platoon officers just out from Britain were lucky to last a few weeks; and they were more often killed or wounded in a matter of days through not knowing when precisely to keep their heads down or how to assess the enemy's strength. One new addition to Right Flank, however, was Frank Waldron from Support Company who had been with the Battalion longer than myself. His anti-tank gun section had knocked out five German tanks at the Battle of Medenine in North Africa and he had been in Support Company ever since. But owing to a quarrel with his new Support Company commander, he had recently found himself back at LOB (left out of battle) where I had caught up with him when hitchhiking back from hospital. He now asked to be allowed to accompany me back to Right Flank to try to 'remake his name'. Frank was still dressed for desert warfare without a steel helmet or indeed without any lethal weapon. He asked me for the loan of one of my extra Bren guns as he thought charging the enemy firing from the hip might be the best way of winning an MC! He said he simply had to get one as otherwise 'everyone in London' would think him 'yellow', having gone through North Africa, Italy and now Germany without a decoration. At the end of the orders group, Frank jokingly told Hugh Rose, who had now taken over from Digby Raeburn as acting company commander, that he was trying to 'get us all brewed up' – and so we set off.

Just outside Kettenburg the Germans opened fire on our two forward platoons and one of their machine-guns enfiladed Frank's forward sections. Frank was badly wounded trying to get over a fence and his platoon sergeant, when laying him on a stretcher, was instantly killed. Frank himself was also hit again when lying on the stretcher; but happily survived.

As reserve platoon I had a grandstand view of what was happening but with the enemy's fire passing well over my head. I could see casualties crumbling to the ground and stretcher-bearers bravely tending them. Our infantry were mostly lying flat or trying to wriggle to shelter behind folds in the ground. Behind them the tanks were putting down smoke and firing belt after belt of Besa straight into the German positions as well as blowing up the houses on either side. Eventually the enemy fire slackened and we started moving forward again. But we were clearly up against a skilled and determined German opposition – not the boy soldiers we had recently been encountering.

My platoon now advanced through Frank's platoon to clear the wood beyond, where we shot some Germans. A German platoon up the road also surrendered to 9 Platoon. The remainder of these German marines had fought bravely considering the amount of tank and artillery fire directed at them. We left some fifteen of them dead or dying. I spoke to one who was being very brave as a terrible scalp wound was being bandaged. A carrier section came in with a further bunch of German prisoners and wounded. This brought the day's tally of prisoners to 250 and we had taken the village of Kettenburg despite such strong resistance.

At 5 p.m. came a further order to advance against the little town of Visselhovede just in front, covering the road towards the major town of Rotenburg. General instructions were to quicken the advance and push on as Visselhovede had already been wrongly reported by the Coldstream battle group to be undefended. We were later to gather from prisoners that there were five fresh German companies of the 2nd Marine Division now positioned around Visselhovede.

One of the platoons in my company was now commanded by a lance-sergeant, formerly an aircraftsman. But one hardly noticed now who was ex-RAF Regiment and who was not; for all firmly identified as Scots Guardsmen. The plan of attack on Visselhovede was to push straight on up the road and link up with the Coldstream battle group somewhere to our right. Right Flank with my platoon in the lead, however, only got half way along the road before we ran into strong fire from German positions. We leapt off our tanks into the nearest ditch where we came under even heavier fire from strong positions along the edge of a wood some 150 yards in front with open fields in between. The Germans also fired several Panzerfausts trying to hit our tanks; but the range was too great – although some landed among my men in the roadside ditch, slightly wounding Sergeant Ross and another man. Observing the flashes and smoke coming from all along the edge of the wood, I estimated that a whole German company was entrenched there and that the best tactic would be for a whole company flanking attack from the right. But it was now getting dark and the attack was called off with an order for all tanks to withdraw into laager at Kettenburg for the night.

Among our wounded to be evacuated was Sergeant McPhee (from Italy), now commanding a platoon who had been hit in the thigh. He was the last of our old sergeants except for Company Sergeant-Major Lindsay, from Dumfriesshire. The latter had been a corporal in the carriers in North Africa; platoon sergeant in Italy; and was now our Company Sergeant-Major. It was characters like these who really kept Right Flank together in these last few days of the war. Lance-Sergeant Ross who was equally outstanding, now therefore became my platoon sergeant.

I was now the only rifle platoon officer left in the company – all the other platoons being commanded by NCOs. Alastair Erskine and I were also the only two rifle platoon officers still surviving who had landed with the Battalion at Salerno. One day we discussed how we had managed to survive. We concluded that the key was our experience in being able to 'read the battle' and also to direct our platoons from the centre rather than from out in front shouting 'Follow me!' in accordance with current 'battle-drill' practices. I could also pride myself on having far less casualties than in any of the other platoons. Another precaution adopted by Alastair and myself was in removing all our officers' insignia, including shoulder stars and MC ribbons, from our battledress tunics. It was not so easy then in this close fighting for the enemy to pick us out as being platoon officers.

Morale was nevertheless surprisingly high considering all the circumstances. Unlike in Italy, there were no cases of soldiers reporting sick without cause. We were obviously now winning the war and there was even an occasional bed to sleep in. Close combat even appeared to be good for morale especially as we thought we were rather better at this than the enemy. A major difference too from Italy was the quick removal of the dead and wounded by stretcher and jeep from the battlefield. We not only had stretcher-bearers following on foot but also ambulance half-tracks flying the Red Cross which the Germans never fired on and even allowed to approach near their positions when evacuating our wounded. In contrast one remembered those four-men stretcher loads coming down the Italian mountains in the pouring rain. It was also the reason why so many of our badly wounded then failed to survive.

At daybreak Right Flank with our Welsh Guards tanks were now to resume the advance into supposedly undefended Visselhovede. The information from XII Corps Headquarters was that the Coldstream battle group operating on a small side road to the east had skirted into the back of Visselhovede and reported seeing no Germans. The Germans defending the front of this small key town protecting Rotenburg were therefore quite wrongly thought to have withdrawn.

At dawn next morning there was thus a great hurry to start. The general plan was for Right Flank to advance into the left of Vissel-hovede, 'G' Company into the centre, and 'F' Company on the right. The latter were also to deal with our enemy in the wood of the night before – if they were still there.

When we were about to move off, the squadron commander of our company/squadron battle group came up and asked me to get my men immediately on top of his tanks preparatory to motoring straight up last night's road past the very wood from which we had been fired on. I do not think he had personally seen what happened. This was anyway 'F' Company's line of advance with 'G' Company to our left and Right Flank to the left again. I expostulated and said this needed a set-piece attack as there was no reason whatsoever to suppose the Germans had withdrawn. Only those in front could know whether they had or had not done so. He became angry and said we were to advance together up the road and that if I did not mount his tanks at once they would continue without us. I therefore said I would be prepared to put my infantry on the second but not on the leading tank, to which he eventually agreed.

As my men had heard this heated argument I felt in honour bound to put myself on the second (i.e. the first infantry-laden) tank where, however, I sat on the left-hand protected side of its turret.

So we set off straight up the road towards the very wood where the Germans had been firmly entrenched but which was really the objective of 'F' Company following behind. The distance narrowed to a hundred yards and still no sign of the enemy. Then the leading tank started to pass alongside the wood itself with the commander's head and shoulders protruding from its turret. Still no German reaction. I now began to feel a complete fool who would have to make a public apology to the Welsh Guards squadron commander.

Suddenly a Panzerfaust sailed through the air from the edge of the wood and hit the turret of the leading tank – but without exploding. The Germans had cunningly let it through to render our infantry better targets. Within seconds a hail of bullets now raked the top of my tank as I hugged the left side of its turret shouting at the tank commander to stop and let us get off. This seemed to take an age. I could not hear the Spandaus firing for the noise of the tank; but could see men reeling around me from the impact of machine-gun bullets. As I was pressed shoulder to shoulder against Sergeant Ross I could even feel bullets hitting him straight in the chest. Our tanks all veered off the tarmac road into the field on the left and so out of Panzerfaust range. Most of my leading section were shot off the tank, landing right under the Germans' noses, including Sergeant Ross who was mortally wounded. I managed to hang on sideways behind the tank turret and then dropped to the ground as it lurched to a standstill. One could then momentarily stand protected by the tank and watch machine gun bullets tearing up a furrow in the turf beside it.

We were, of course, still under positive orders *not* to attack the wood which was 'F' Company's objective; but anyway we could not possibly have done so. We had somehow to extricate ourselves and move on to our proper line of advance on the left-hand side of Visselhovede. In all the noise it was difficult to communicate with my tank commander whose turret was understandably half-closed. I eventually got two tanks run together to form a bullet-proof screen between us and the enemy. My platoon then bypassed them within a hundred yards. The other two platoons of Right Flank and also those of 'G' Company following behind gave them a still wider berth, keeping, like us, to the leeward side of their tanks which formed a shield between them and the enemy.

It was for 'F' Company to follow up and deal with the German company in the wood when any still-surviving wounded could be rescued. With the Germans at such short range we only managed to get two slightly wounded propped up on the side of one tank behind its turret. In the event 'F' Company had later to mount a full-scale company attack supported by tanks from the front and ending with a fierce charge on the large numbers of entrenched enemy, most of whom died in their trenches.

With the Welsh Guards' tanks we now moved over on to our own proper line of advance on the left, where another road led into Visselhovede. There was no sign here at first of any Germans and so we did not even dig in. We also heard, to our amazement, that our battle group headquarters were now somewhere in front of us, having installed themselves in the main street of the town. They had apparently motored straight in from this direction on Corps information that there were no enemy in Visselhovede. All company commanders were then summoned to an orders group. These included Hugh Rose, who only got within a quarter of a mile of headquarters in our company carrier before he was fired on. Guardsman Chadwick, DCM, (of tobacco factory fame) was driving the carrier and promptly turned it completely around in its tracks and over the side of a railway embankment. Unfortunately there were also Germans on the other side who, with the contents of the carrier now revealed, put a burst of fire right into the driver's compartment killing our two old signallers Corporals Perks and Connell. The former was the last of the old corporals and had won the MM for mending telephone lines under fire at Minturno. Hugh Rose and Chadwick then jumped over the other side of the carrier and managed to escape.

Meanwhile around our crossroads to the south we knew nothing at first of these happenings. I was now in effect commanding the company. Our Squadron Commander suddenly informed me that he had just received a wireless message that Scots/Welsh Group Headquarters were themselves under direct attack by the enemy and we must go straight up the road to rescue them. This at first caused us some amusement – we thought that Battalion HQ must just be 'flapping' on account of some stray shots. We set off down the road riding at first on top of the tanks; but as we approached the outskirts of the town I insisted that this time we be allowed to dismount. We then moved in front of or to the side of our tanks to protect them from Panzerfausts. The gardens here behind the houses seemed to be swarming with Germans, none of whom were dug in. Indeed they appeared to have just moved into position.

I was foolish enough at one point to turn my back (not a good thing to do in street fighting) while I was speaking to Corporal Stewart. His look of blank amazement and the speed with which he suddenly brought his rifle up to the aim made me realise what was up. Without turning I jumped sideways; but so did the German who was about to shoot me in the back!

Apparently what had happened was that a whole battalion of the 7th Marine Grenadiers, determined not to give up without a fight (and no one as yet having actually attacked them), had merely moved into Visselhovede from the woods to the west. With no initial opposition they then quickly occupied the main street where our joint battle group HQ had only one platoon of 'G' Company to protect them. The latter were surrounded and sustained about a dozen casualties. Our HQ tanks were also unable to move or fire for fear of hitting our infantry. Two of our mortar carriers were set on fire by Panzerfausts. The headquarters hotel building itself was surrounded and the Adjutant was reduced to firing his revolver out of the back window.

We meanwhile advanced up the road on either side of our tanks, firing at Germans and also taking prisoners as we went. About a hundred yards short of the headquarters hotel, we reached a newly constructed road-block where the bullets really began to fly. Leaving my own platoon to consolidate, I sent one of the other platoons down the right-hand side clearing houses from the back. I took the remainder to try and force our way through to the headquarters hotel itself. One of my men was shot just outside its window; we entered from the garden side where a German Spandau shot another two of my men. We were thus only fourteen strong when we reached headquarters. They looked greatly relieved to see us. The more senior officers were sitting mournfully around a table as in some erstwhile outpost of Empire with the hostile natives just about to burst in on them.

Our tank/infantry group now took over 100 prisoners in as many yards of group headquarters. Realising that the game was really up, they came pouring out of all the surrounding cellars with their hands above their heads. I was cursing some of my platoon for looting rather than house clearing when I discovered that I was wearing two pairs of captured binoculars myself! The total bag of prisoners for the day reached 400. Chief prize was Colonel Jordan and most of the staff of the 5th Marine Panzer Grenadiers whom we took prisoner just down the road. They may have been there all along when our joint group headquarters astonishingly moved in beside them. One had to give credit to these German Marines still loyal to Admiral Doenitz and their country, who without any tank support and in the heart of western Germany had nearly overrun our battalion headquarters.

We found billets for the night in the same street. I was just about to turn in when Hugh Rose, who had now returned, said he was very sorry to hear about Alastair Erskine and had I heard? I certainly had not; but was now about to do so. Alastair had been attempting with a section of 'G' Company to get through to battalion headquarters from the opposite direction to ourselves. His elder brother was the intelligence officer also under siege. At one point Alastair's platoon had to take shelter from enemy fire between a tank and a street wall. But a Spandau mounted in a jutting out window was able to fire straight up the street and hit the whole section including Alastair with one burst. He might have survived if they had been able to extricate him straight away; but the stretcher-bearers were also machine-gunned and in the end he died in the ambulance on his way to a casualty clearing station.

He was an outstanding soldier, intending to be a regular. We had also been at the same school together and he was the only other surviving rifle platoon officer who had landed at Salerno. The real tragedy was that the Commanding Officer had just arranged that he be relieved and sent as a liaison officer to Divisional Headquarters the very next day.

I locked myself into a separate room for the night and would not come out for anyone. I was totally exhausted and frankly had had quite enough for the moment – as indeed had Alastair Erskine himself before he was killed.

Next day 53rd Division came up to take over our positions and we re-embussed in our TCLs to continue the advance on Rotenburg once our engineers had filled in the craters caused by a blown bridge. The defence of this large communication centre had really hinged on the German marines at Visselhovde. We lined up along the road while 'G' Company led the way and the Coldstream tank/infantry group attacked from the east. It was a day of intermittent sparkling sunshine and rain. My platoon sat in the back of their TCL singing a song of their own composition. Its final chorus (accompanied by the stamping of feet) was:

We won't go to Heaven in a TCL
We won't go to Heaven when we die!

They were marvellous but, for the present, I could not share their brand of humour. The attack was a walkover as the town was full of German military hospitals and its mayor promptly offered to surrender to our battle group. He was carried back into the town with his white flag flying on top of one of our tanks. However, the local military commander was of a different view so a few token shots had first to be fired.

The German troops around Rotenburg were ordinary Wehrmacht and, as was occurring now over the whole of central Germany, were surrendering in droves. The Battalion took several hundred that day with hardly a casualty. 250 surrendered to one platoon of 'G' Company. This was a situation similar to what was now taking place all over the south, where the Americans were rapidly advancing against diminishing opposition; but this was our first experience in the north of such wholesale surrenders without military engagement. Prisoners came pouring out of the houses in every stage of undress and dejection. Our companies cleared the town by sections; but there was no proper fighting. 'G' Company rescued one of their own men in a military hospital who had been wounded and taken prisoner a fortnight before. He had been well looked after. The only two casualties were in my platoon when, at the far end of the town, my leading section bumped into a German platoon position facing in the opposite direction. Some Germans came out of a house, perhaps to surrender, but got fired at so they disappeared back into their positions and a Spandau then opened up, wounding Corporal Stewart and another man.

At this juncture a civilian came cycling past the leading tank troop and continued even when the troop sergeant shouted at him to stop. The tank sergeant let him get a hundred yards on and then riddled him with Besa. He collapsed dead over his bicycle just in front of one of the hospitals. A nurse came running out to him, but seeing that he was dead, ran in again.

We had three Wasp flamethrowers attached to my company under command of a sergeant who kept pestering me to be allowed to have a go at the enemy – never as yet having had an opportunity to do so. He lined up his three Wasps behind some outhouses which separated us from the enemy, put down a huge wall of flame for thirty seconds and then everyone charged in through the smoke, yelling at the German soldiers to come out. Only one of them was killed and the remaining score of prisoners were extremely scared, even shrinking at first from my offer of a lift back on top of the *flammenwerfer*.

The 53rd Infantry Division were now left to complete the mopping up of the town of Rotenburg and its surrounding countryside, while four days later I found myself 'dug away' at Divisional Headquarters as liaison officer in the very post that had previously been arranged for Alastair Erskine. I certainly needed a change, although the war was now nearly over, with rumours of Hitler's death in his Berlin bunker and the Swedish Count Bernadotte said to be engaged in peace negotiations. There was still some spirited fighting at Westertville and Osterville involving Left Flank followed by a considerable amount of shelling. The very last day on which the Battalion was in action was 27 April 1945, when among those killed by shelling was Guardsman G. McKeard who had been with 2SG continuously from 1940 – first in the Desert, then in Italy and now Western Germany.

I was quite glad not to be in the front line at this final stage, as many of the German troops in these northern parts now directed by Admiral Doenitz from Cuxhaven were by no means dispirited and had been asking for special terms owing to their still formidable armament. Having survived for so long I did not fancy meeting my end in some trivial mopping up operation.

On 3 May 1945 our Corps Commander, General Horrocks, ordered no further advance beyond the line of the Oste Canal, as the terms of unconditional surrender were now being negotiated.

It was a satisfying contrast, to be now acting as temporary ADC to Major-General Adair commanding the Guards Armoured Division and to be present in the operational tent when General Goltsch, commanding German Corps EMS, came in to surrender. His corps comprised our recent opponents, the 6th and 7th Parachutist Divisions, and also the 15th Panzergrenadiers who had previously confronted 201 Guards Brigade on Monte Camino.

We had to wait in the tent until General Ritchie commanding XII Corps arrived. Some of the German generals were now trying to obtain special terms, so they maintained, as respected old opponents. General Horrocks replied that he was a professional soldier and that he had fought the Germans as Corps Commander for three years, during which time he had gained a profound respect for them as soldiers. But having just seen Sandbostel concentration camp he was extremely angry; and in future all his orders would be given without mercy: 'I repeat,' he said, 'without mercy.' Instantly the German generals started protesting that the Wehrmacht were not connected with the Waffen SS. General Horrocks replied that he had seen Wehrmacht soldiers on duty at the gates of Sandbostel, and that was enough for him. Silence ensued.

I had also seen the piles of corpses through the wire of Sandbostel which had just been liberated.

Another day, as a junior staff officer, I was able to motor through Bremen to observe six square miles of brick rubble flattened by British 'carpet bombing'. In the centre there was not a single house or building left standing. Another day I saw the whole of Hamburg in a similar state of total devastation; indeed one could hardly drive between the mountains of rubble. All the civilian population had sheltered underground. A sullen sense of German identity still seemed to have survived this saturation bombing. Every canal that one passed was choked with barges sunk by the RAF in the last few days of the war now that there was no opposition. Our Spitfires had simply flown up and down, machine-gunning the helpless barges regardless of the future supply problems they were causing.

One day I was sent with another staff officer to arrange the details for the handover of the armament of the 6th and 7th German Parachute Divisions. These were assembled on an aerodrome near Cuxhaven, where the parachutists had already surrendered to the Coldstream battle group. We found the tarmac covered with their self-propelled guns – a formidable sight; but there were no tanks. Indeed when one came to think of it, unlike at Salerno, we had not seen a single German tank during our recent advance – only self-propelled guns.

Another day I took a scout car to Cuxhaven which had been occupied unopposed by the Scots/Welsh group. Here a part of the surrendered German Fleet was still anchored. There were some destroyers and E Boats but no cruisers; tied up alongside the quay, however, were submarines which still had their crews aboard. There was also a floating brothel nearby, full of females. Seeing one submarine commander standing on deck, I asked if I could see round his vessel which he readily allowed me to do. We climbed down the ladder of his conning tower into the lower part of the hold where his entire crew were sitting silently in rows. These were his 'platoon' of submariners to whom he was obviously devoted. They promptly stopped talking and all stared at me sullenly until eventually I thought it was time to leave. As I reached the deck, the commander asked me whether I could arrange for him and his crew to be kept together to fight in the continuing war against the Japanese. I said I did not think it likely that I could make any such arrangement!

Since the Battalion had crossed the Rhine a month before, the rifle companies had sustained the worst of the casualties with 17 platoon officers killed or wounded and 223 other ranks. Right Flank alone had lost 95. During the war as a whole the Battalion had now lost 113 officers killed or wounded and 1,246 other ranks – more than in the First World War.

On Sunday 6 May 1945 I attended the Scots/Welsh Group's Service of Remembrance in the old Lutheran Church at Stade. The official German surrender had been marked the previous day with a *feu de joie* from the Corps artillery, firing off all their unused live ammunition. So the war in the West was really over.

The church was of mellow red brick and had stood throughout the centuries. First we heard the National Anthem played by an amateur organist, followed by prayers officially recommended by the Archbishop of Canterbury. Their refrain was: 'Thine is the Victory,

O Lord, not mine.' The congregation replied at the end of each prayer: 'We thank thee O Lord.'

Our respected padre, the Revd David Whiteford, then stepped down and the two Commanding Officers of the Scots/Welsh group presided over the remainder of the service, which was more of a memorial to our dead. Standing by the altar each Commanding Officer read out the long list of his battalion's dead in a voice deep with emotion. The Last Post was then sounded by trumpet from outside the great west door, to be followed by two minutes' silence. Then Pipe Major Bain started playing a Scottish lament on his pipes from beside the altar – the 'Flowers of the Forest, that fought aye the foremost, the prime of our land, lie cauld in the clay'.

His piping brought tears to many eyes as he marched slowly through the west door and down the hill, his notes growing fainter and fainter. One thought of graves on the Italian mountains and now along the German roads. But as the piping became more distant it seemed as if the spring breezes played tricks with the lament so that it echoed back sounding more like a Scottish reel. One thought of laughter as the sun went down and of songs around the brew can fires; of Corporal Bryson trying to catch old Gallene in the Italian rain, of Sergeant-Major Lumsden roaring drunk at Hogmanay; of laughter in the back of the TCLs and of Support Company trying to pretend there was not a war on.

The 2nd Battalion Scots Guards – they were a terrible mob; but I would not have fought in any other.

Index

Adair, Major-General Allan, 146

Bain, Pipe Major, 148
Balfour, Captain Anthony, 64, 72, 73, 74, 93
Benson, Guardsman, 109
Berridge, Dick, 131
Bowen-Colthurst, Paddy, 65, 73, 83
Bruce, Guardsman, 123
Bryson, Corporal 'Swill', 87, 97, 99, 148
Buckle, Dickie, 58-9

Chadwick, Guardsman, 36-7, 38, 80, 109, 122, 141-2
Clark, General Mark (USA), 15, 61
Clowes, Lieutenant-Colonel Henry, 103, 136, 144
Coke, Major Richard, 82
Coldstream Guards, 14, 69, 110, 123-4, 139-40
Connell, Corporal, 142
Coyle, Guardsman, 39-40

de Soissons, Victor, 115, 116, 128, 129, 133
Drake, Robert, 28, 29

Erskine, The Hon. Alastair, 102, 107, 139, 143-4, 145

'Feathers', see Steuart-Fothringham
Fraser, Drill-Sergeant, 108
Fraser, Ian, 38, 41, 42, 45, 46-55, 58

Gascoigne, Brigadier Julian (Grenadiers), 70, 78
Gow, Graham, 118
Greenwood, Lieutenant-Quartermaster, 92
Grenadier Guards, 14, 28, 32, 69, 71, 81, 110
Griffiths, Hugh (Welsh Guards), 132-3

Harris, Lieutenant-Colonel F.H.H.B., 'Boy', 92-94, 98
Horrocks, General Sir Brian, 18, 121, 146
Houldsworth, Major Sammy, 60
Household Cavalry, 125
Hutchison, Sergeant-Major, 35, 36, 92

Irish Guards, 110, 111-13

'Joe Plush', see Wilson

Leese, General Sir Oliver, 101
Lindsay, Company Sergeant-Major, 109, 138-9
Lumsden, Sergeant-Major, 31, 116, 148
Lyttelton, Humphrey, 21

Macphee, Sergeant, 97, 116, 130, 138-9
Macrae, Major Johnny, 16, 61
Mannock, Tony, 126
McCreery, General Sir Richard, 18

McKeard, Guardsman, 145
Moncreiffe of That Ilk, Sir Iain, 88
Murphy, Guardsman, 39-40

Perks, Corporal, 142

Raeburn, Major Digby, 94, 128, 130,
    137, 142
Ritchie, General, 146
Rivers-Bulkeley, Major Bobby, 30,
    31, 33, 58
Rose, Captain Hugh, 137, 141, 142,
    143
Ross, Sergeant, 138, 139, 140-1

Stewart, Corporal, 132, 142, 145
Stewart, Sergeant, 34, 35, 36
Steuart-Fothringham, Major P.,
    'Feathers', 91

Swinton, John, 118, 136

Taylor, Lieutenant-Colonel Guy,
    18-19, 22, 27, 31, 60, 61-2, 67, 70,
    71, 74, 78, 93
Templer, General Sir Gerald, 92
Torrance, Neil, 118

Watson, 'Blondie', 27
Waldron, Captain Frank, 91, 120-1,
    137, 138
Welsh Guards, 110, 115, 121-3, 124,
    127, 130, 134, 136, 139, 141, 142,
    148
White, Sergeant, 128-9
Whiteford, Revd David, 148
Wilson, Sergeant 'Joe Plush', 87, 88,
    94, 123, 124, 127, 128, 147